Full Stack Web Development with Backbone.js

Patrick Mulder

Beijing · Cambridge · Farnham · Köln · Sebastopol · Tokyo

Full Stack Web Development with Backbone.js

by Patrick Mulder

Printed in the United States of America.

Published by O'Reilly Media, Inc., 1005 Gravenstein Highway North, Sebastopol, CA 95472.

O'Reilly books may be purchased for educational, business, or sales promotional use. Online editions are also available for most titles (*http://safaribooksonline.com*). For more information, contact our corporate/institutional sales department: 800-998-9938 or *corporate@oreilly.com*.

Editors: Simon St. Laurent and Brian MacDonald	**Indexer:** Judy McConville
Production Editor: Kara Ebrahim	**Cover Designer:** Randy Comer
Copyeditor: Jasmine Kwityn	**Interior Designer:** David Futato
Proofreader: Amanda Kersey	**Illustrator:** Rebecca Demarest

June 2014:   First Edition

Revision History for the First Edition:

2014-06-09:   First release

2014-08-15:   Second release

2015-01-16:   Third release

See *http://oreilly.com/catalog/errata.csp?isbn=9781449370985* for release details.

ISBN: 978-1-449-37098-5

[LSI]

Table of Contents

Preface

Web users demand intuitive and responsive interfaces for tracking their finances and browsing catalogs. Unlike desktop or system applications, where interfaces are mostly built with flavors of C, C++, or Java, today's web browsers only run JavaScript natively. But the same patterns that make graphical user interfaces successful on different platforms apply to JavaScript as well.

Many communities have formed around experimenting and developing ideas for the model-view-controller (MVC) pattern with JavaScript. It seems like every day there is a new idea about how MVC in web browsers should look and why other ideas won't work for you.

In these turbulent times, the Backbone.js library stands out like a lighthouse. Unlike other approaches to JavaScript MVC, Backbone.js is very small and flexible. However, the main difference of Backbone.js compared to its peers is the Backbone "ecosystem." Backbone's philosophy of staying small gave birth to many plug-ins and a multitude of different, and some unique, use cases.

This rich ecosystem makes learning and understanding Backbone hard. If you are new to JavaScript, or if you have only built server-side web applications, you are faced with a number of problems. How do you combine views and the data layer with JavaScript? How do you abstract away JavaScript dependencies, such as Backbone plug-ins? How do you best serve and deploy JavaScript assets? But also, where is the "controller" in Backbone, or when are they used?

Answering these questions is one goal of this book. But Backbone.js really starts to shine when you learn to explore and engage with its rich ecosystem. First, there are many plug-ins for Backbone.js that can help you solve advanced UI problems. Second, build tools can help you to be more productive and also enable you to reuse ideas on both the client and server. This is my second goal: I want to show how a full-stack JavaScript application with Backbone.js can be built with the help of JavaScript modules, workflow automation, and the use of Backbone plug-ins. For the backend, you will learn about basic API design ideas as well as perspectives on authentication.

Maybe you will be intimated by the variety of tools that you can use to develop Backbone.js web applications. The Backbone.js ecosystem is quite large, so not all choices of tools will work for you. However, I hope this book will help you to decide which tools will work best for the particular app you are working on.

If your JavaScript programming skills are a bit rusty, entering client-side application development can be a daunting adventure. I hope to provide a sort of basecamp from where you can explore different directions to build interactions within browsers and help you to understand the benefits of separating interface from application state.

In summary, we'll cover:

- How to quickly get started with a Backbone.js sandbox
- How to manage data and state with Backbone.js models and collections
- How to work with advanced view templates and Handlebars
- How to use Backbone.js to browse data sources from an API
- How to authenticate and authorize client-side interactions
- How to improve productivity of a team with workflow automation and Backbone frameworks

Who This Book Is For

This book is written for readers coming from one of these backgrounds:

- You are a backend developer with some experience in rendering web pages on the server. You are maybe impressed by the fast feedback from browser applications, or you want to build advanced browser interfaces for navigating and editing data in the browser.
- You are a frontend developer with interests in single-page web applications or interactive widgets in web browsers. You maybe found jQuery not meeting your goals anymore and are looking to learn what Backbone.js is about.
- You are a product manager or team lead that is responsible for making technology choices. If you want to understand where Backbone.js and JavaScript fit in your technolgoy stack, this book is for you.

Building single-page web applications involves more than just questions around interfaces, so this book also discusses basics of JavaScript modules, build approaches, and API backends. When scanning the table of contents this book, you might discover that JavaScript offers a number of interesting options.

Hopefully this book can show paths to structure web applications in a new way, toward friendlier and more scalable web applications. This book will be especially interesting to developers who want to learn approaches for using a user interfaces as a service, where frontend and backend services can be maintained and deployed independently.

Who This Book Is Not For

With Backbone.js, you have a lot of freedom to control interactions with documents based on JavaScript. The scope of the book is *not* avoiding JavaScript in the first place.

Other frameworks to build interactive documents such as Angular.js or Ember provide more abstractions and a high amount of "sugar" to build interfaces. However, the philosophy of this book is to pull in abstractions and dependencies when needed, and not start with those in the first place. This book should provide Backbone's viewpoint on when and why certain abstractions are useful.

Related to maintainable and scalable application design is testing. Testing JavaScript applications with, for example, Jasmine or command-line tools is discussed in other specialized books and will be mentioned where appropriate.

Although the ideas from Backbone.js have quickly diffused into very interesting realms, such as highly interactive maps, system applications, browser extension, and hybrid applications for mobile phones, it is not possible to discuss all of these.

You will work mainly with the browser, a text editor, and the command line. If you prefer integrated development environments (IDEs), any one with support for JavaScript will do, such as Webstorms from Jetbrains or a version of Visual Studio with Node plug-ins. Also, Netbeans and Eclipse should support basic web development with JavaScript and HTML.

If you are on a Windows machine that does not support a Unix command line, you might want to install Cygwin or a virtual machine (VM) running Unix so that you can better follow along with the examples.

What This Book Will Do for You

The first goal of this book is to help you understand the different use cases of Backbone.js. Since its first release in 2010, Backbone.js has built up a good reputation for improving the development of client-side web applications. There are a number of interesting projects and companies that use Backbone.js. For example, Walmart uses Backbone.js as the core library of its mobile shopping cart. Airbnb uses Backbone.js to let users and search engines browse available travel accomodations. DocumentCloud has built a document screening service with Backbone.js. There are many more examples, and you can find an interesting overview in the Examples section of the Backbone.js documentation (*http://backbonejs.org/#examples*).

Second, this book should help you climb the learning curve for getting things done on the client side. Many books target JavaScript frontend developers and leave out those having built server-side web applications. Other books stop the discussion when Backbone.js can be put to practical use in real applications.

Hopefully this book can provide a bridge from client-side to server-side concepts and help you understand the advantages of the Backbone ecosystem. You can then adopt a mind-set for JavaScript applications in general, on the client or in combination with server-side JavaScript.

Why I Wrote This Book

Working as a Ruby on Rails developer, I observed the JavaScript and NodeJS developments with some skepticism. After all, Ruby land created a lot of innovations that contribute to the happiness and productivity of developers and businesses.

But as with any other framework or maturing application, code bases become harder to maintain, and it is difficult to redesign applications toward mobile clients and maintain smooth interactions with data. It is here where the JavaScript community is heavily experimenting and solutions for building scalable architectures for mobile web applications emerge.

However, the user interface is just a layer in a larger application stack, and the design of interactions takes more than just patching existing web applications. JavaScript is a good choice to drive an application stack for web interactions, but it also brings new demands on concepts and data schemas. The goal of this book is to show how client-side applications can evolve from basic interaction ideas, and how more modular and maintainable web applications can be built.

Other Resources

To understand the perspectives in this book, you need a sound knowledge of JavaScript, browsers, and DOM manipulation, as well as a basic knowledge of web applications. Also, there are a number of resources available to go deeper into single-page application development.

The JavaScript Language

To learn JavaScript, there are a number of good resources available:

JavaScript Garden (http://bonsaiden.github.io/JavaScript-Garden/)
    This is an open source resource on programming in JavaScript. This online guide is a good place to turn to for improving your understanding of quirky aspects of the language without consulting a book.

JavaScript: The Good Parts by Douglas Crockford (O'Reilly/Yahoo! Press, 2008)
> This book is a gentle introduction to the grammar and semantics of the JavaScript language. It can be read quite quickly and is referenced from many other sources too. So, if you are new to JavaScript, this book might be good to have.

JavaScript: The Definitive Guide, 6th Edition, by David Flanagan (O'Reilly, 2011)
> Considered a bible for JavaScript development, this book discusses in detail the roles JavaScript plays in browsers and for server-side applications.

Speaking JavaScript: An In-Depth Guide for Programmers by Axel Rauschmayer (O'Reilly, 2014)
> This book provides a complete introduction to JavaScript, as well as a good overview on its evolution and best practices for using it.

For readers who want to look further into JavaScript, there are a number of other interesting books. For example, *JavaScript Patterns* by Stoyan Stefanov (O'Reilly, 2010), *Learning JavaScript Design Patterns* by Addy Osmani (O'Reilly, 2012), and *JavaScript Cookbook* by Shelley Powers (O'Reilly, 2010) contain a lot of helpful patterns that can help you to be a better JavaScript developer.

jQuery and the DOM

For readers who need to grasp the basics for working with jQuery and the DOM, *JavaScript and jQuery: The Missing Manual* by David Sawyer McFarland (O'Reilly, 2011) will be helpful.

For readers who want to explore further advanced effects with DOM nodes, *Supercharged JavaScript Graphics* by Raffaele Cecco (O'Reilly, 2011) will be a very interesting read. This book discusses a lot of nice details on rendering and animation of DOM nodes in the browser.

Other Backbone.js Resources

If you want to consult additional resources that discuss Backbone.js specifically, the following list should get you started:

Developing Backbone.js Applications (O'Reilly, 2013)
> With this book (also sometimes listed as *Backbone Fundamentals*), Addy Osmani has written one of the first books on Backbone.js. His book starts with an in-depth discussion of the MVC pattern and continues with a number of different Backbone examples, such as an editor of Todo lists and a small library editor. Addy's book might be a good companion to this book, because it serves as more of a reference book, unlike this book's more specialized approach that focuses on one particular application. Addy concentrates more on frontend development, while this book also includes ideas and concepts for backend development.

Thoughtbot's Backbone.js on Rails (https://learn.thoughtbot.com/products/1-backbone-js-on-rails)

> This self-published book is great from a Ruby on Rails perspective, because it includes a lot of Ruby code examples that are necessary to drive a Backbone.js frontend in Rails. It also does a nice job in discussing Jasmine and Capybara for frontend testing.

Building Backbone Plugins (https://leanpub.com/building-backbone-plugins)

> Consult this book written by Derick Bailey and Jerome Gravel-Niquet if you want to delve more into writing Backbone plug-ins and reusable code in general. Also, with the Pragmatic Bookshelf's *Hands-on Backbone.js* (*http://pragprog.com/screencasts/v-dback/hands-on-backbone-js*), Derick has published a number of screencasts that might help more audio-visual inclined learners.

BackboneRails.com (http://www.backbonerails.com/)

> Brian Mann's screencasts provide a great discussion of concepts and examples for developing client-side applications together with Ruby on Rails.

Last but not least, the source code of Backbone itself and of many Backbone plug-ins are good places to improve your understanding of Backbone details. The Backbone annotated source code is at *http://backbonejs.org/docs/backbone.html*, and Backbone plug-ins can be found via *http://backplug.io/* and *http://backboneindex.com/*.

API References

Additionally, the documentation of JavaScript and the APIs will be helpful:

- JavaScript general documentation (*https://developer.mozilla.org/en/docs/Web/JavaScript*)
- Documentation of jQuery (*http://api.jquery.com/*)
- Underscore (*http://underscorejs.org/*)
- Backbone (*http://backbonejs.org/*)

Conventions Used in This Book

The following typographical conventions are used in this book:

Italic

> Indicates new terms, URLs, email addresses, filenames, and file extensions.

Constant width

> Used for program listings, as well as within paragraphs to refer to program elements such as variable or function names, databases, data types, environment variables, statements, and keywords.

Constant width bold

> Shows commands or other text that should be typed literally by the user.

Constant width italic

> Shows text that should be replaced with user-supplied values or by values determined by context.

 This element signifies a tip or suggestion.

 This element signifies a general note.

 This element indicates a warning or caution.

Feedback and Code Examples

As Backbone.js has its roots in open source software development, feedback and discussion about the presented material is highly appreciated.

The book website (*http://pipefishbook.com*) will collect all libraries that are mentioned in this book. Also, there will be references to interesting blog posts about the topics from the book.

As the book examples will be hosted on GitHub, you can either leave an issue on GitHub under *https://github.com/pipefishbook/pipefishbook.github.io*, or send an email to *in fo@pipefishbook.com*.

Using Code Examples

As just noted, supplemental material (code examples, exercises, etc.) is available for download at *https://github.com/pipefishbook*.

This book is here to help you get your job done. In general, if example code is offered with this book, you may use it in your programs and documentation. You do not need to contact us for permission unless you're reproducing a significant portion of the code. For example, writing a program that uses several chunks of code from this book does not require permission. Selling or distributing a CD-ROM of examples from O'Reilly books does require permission. Answering a question by citing this book and quoting example code does not require permission. Incorporating a significant amount of example code from this book into your product's documentation does require permission.

We appreciate, but do not require, attribution. An attribution usually includes the title, author, publisher, and ISBN. For example: "*Developing Web Applications with Backbone.js* by Patrick Mulder (O'Reilly). Copyright 2014 Patrick Mulder, 978-1-449-37098-5."

If you feel your use of code examples falls outside fair use or the permission given above, feel free to contact us at *permissions@oreilly.com*.

Safari® Books Online

 *Safari Books Online* is an on-demand digital library that delivers expert content in both book and video form from the world's leading authors in technology and business.

Technology professionals, software developers, web designers, and business and creative professionals use Safari Books Online as their primary resource for research, problem solving, learning, and certification training.

Safari Books Online offers a range of plans and pricing for enterprise, government, education, and individuals.

Members have access to thousands of books, training videos, and prepublication manuscripts in one fully searchable database from publishers like O'Reilly Media, Prentice Hall Professional, Addison-Wesley Professional, Microsoft Press, Sams, Que, Peachpit Press, Focal Press, Cisco Press, John Wiley & Sons, Syngress, Morgan Kaufmann, IBM Redbooks, Packt, Adobe Press, FT Press, Apress, Manning, New Riders, McGraw-Hill, Jones & Bartlett, Course Technology, and hundreds more. For more information about Safari Books Online, please visit us online.

How to Contact Us

Please address comments and questions concerning this book to the publisher:

O'Reilly Media, Inc.
1005 Gravenstein Highway North
Sebastopol, CA 95472
800-998-9938 (in the United States or Canada)
707-829-0515 (international or local)
707-829-0104 (fax)

We have a web page for this book, where we list errata, examples, and any additional information. You can access this page at *http://bit.ly/dwa-backbone*.

To comment or ask technical questions about this book, send email to *bookques tions@oreilly.com*.

For more information about our books, courses, conferences, and news, see our website at *http://www.oreilly.com*.

Find us on Facebook: *http://facebook.com/oreilly*

Follow us on Twitter: *http://twitter.com/oreillymedia*

Watch us on YouTube: *http://www.youtube.com/oreillymedia*

Acknowledgments

This book wouldn't have been possible without the help of many hands. First, there were the JavaScript pair programming sessions I did with Béla Varga, who is involved in a number of communities for JavaScript development (MunichJS, Coding Dojo), and helped me a lot changing my Ruby-developer biased view on JavaScript.

I want to thank Andrea Notari, Daniele Bertella, and Aurélie Mercier for investing time in a side project that led to experimenting with Backbone.js in the first place. We are trying to make digital work more accessible and transparent.

Thanks for valuable feedback and discussion from Lucas Dohmen, Michael Hackstein, Mathias Lafeldt, Radoslav Stankov, Colin Megill, Eric Trom, Ryan Eastridge, Mike Dvorkin, Martin Gausby, Jeremy Morrell, Jean Carlos Menino, Axel Rauschmayer, Philip Fehre, Roman Sladeczek, Laust Rud Jacobson, Yi Cao, Dave Cadwallader, Nikhilesh Katakam, Patrick Dubroy, Ted Han, Jeremy Ashkenas, Jason Crawford, Peter de Croos, Adam Krebs, Tim Griesser, Sara Robinson, Kevin Sweeney, Petka Antonov, Gorgi Kosev, Marco Ricardo Castañeda, and Stephen McGrath.

Thanks to Dominik Oslizlo for sharing helpful feedback on interface design.

I want to thank my colleagues at Fidor and the people I met at meetups and user groups for supporting me during the project, asking questions or providing helpful directions.

I want to thank my friends and family, who let me write and experiment with JavaScript while I could have been enjoying their company.

If the essence of writing is rewriting, I want to thank my reviewers and editors for helping me during that process of improving the manuscript. A special thanks to my technical reviewers Manuela Mitterdorfer, Garrett Allen, Josh Habdas, Will Mruzek, Sam Saccone, and Jake Buob of MojoTech. Your feedback raised many interesting questions, and I hope that you like the final outcome.

Special thanks to my editor Brian MacDonald at O'Reilly. Your patience and feedback during the writing process were greatly appreciated.

Also, I want to thank Simon St. Laurent and Meg Blanchette for the initial supporting work for this book at O'Reilly. For providing great support in the last stages, I want to thank Jasmine Kwityn and Kara Ebrahim.

Last, I want to thank Béatrice for her love and sense for aesthetics outside of the digital world.

CHAPTER 1

The Bigger Picture

The goal of this first chapter is to provide an introduction to the Backbone.js application environment. It focuses mainly on packages of JavaScript, how to fetch these from the command line, and how to bundle many JavaScript files into one single file.

To learn about the ideas behind Backbone.js, you want to manage as few abstractions as possible. This is why we'll use Node and the command line as our main working environment for the first few chapters. Later in this book, you will meet Yeoman, RequireJS, and Grunt, which automate workflow for JavaScript projects.

If you prefer to skip the command-line ideas for now, and you want to get started with the browser and UX topics directly, you might want to read Chapter 2 first. However, you should return to this chapter afterward so that you can learn more about JavaScript modules and bundling JavaScript for the browser.

In sum, the goal in this chapter is to enter development with JavaScript modules, and we will touch on the following:

- Getting Backbone.js via npm, via a content delivery network (CDN) or from the project site
- Basic bundling of JavaScript applications with Browserify and Stitch
- Common use cases for the CommonJS module format

Before You Get Started

Before you can build Backbone.js applications, it is very important that you know some basic abstractions to work with multiple JavaScript files at once.

There are two reasons:

- You will need to fetch a number of JavaScript dependencies to get going with Backbone.js web applications.
- The view and data layer in Backbone.js applications are generally broken up into separate JavaScript modules.

Bundling JavaScript for the browser is an important topic with many options. A related question is this: how can you organize your JavaScript dependencies and share your projects with others? To follow the answers of this book, you will need a working Node.js setup.

If you don't yet feel comfortable with JavaScript or haven't set up Node.js, you might want to look at the JavaScript refresher in Appendix A; you will find some instructions to set up Node.js.

Backbonify Your Stack

Like Lego, the philosophy of Backbone.js is centered on combining small building blocks that do one thing well. As an introduction, you'll see some of the simplest ways to work with Backbone.js in this chapter.

Besides Backbone.js, you need to fetch two additional libraries to get started. Underscore.js is a fixed dependency for Backbone.js and will help you with filtering and sorting data, as well as working with arrays and functions.

Second, you need a library for manipulating the Document Object Model (DOM). One of the most popular libraries for DOM manipulation is jQuery, but there is also Zepto.js for mobile use cases or Cheerio for server-side DOM manipulation.

So, how can we import these libraries into the web application? There are several ways:

- Fetching local copies by using a package manager, such as npm
- Working with remote references, or CDN networks
- Fetching local copies by downloading the libraries manually

Using npm

If you want to use Node.js, and we will be using it a lot in this book, you can fetch Backbone.js with Node's package manager, or npm.

npm is one of the most important command-line tools in Node. With npm (*http://npmjs.org*), you can quickly access more than 60,000 JavaScript modules. Although npm has its roots on the server side, you can use it for developing browser web applications, too, as we will see later in this chapter.

JavaScript modules will be mentioned a few times in this book. You can think of modules as small code libraries that bundle some functionality. Modules prevent us from reinventing wheels without falling prey to copy-and-paste code. If you are looking for certain functions, it makes sense to search *http://npmjs.org* and play with solutions from other programmers.

First, if you start work on a new project, it makes sense to initialize the project directory as follows:

```
$ npm init
```

You'll get asked a number of questions about your project. You can leave most parts empty for new projects, if you are unsure of the answers when you're first starting out. The important point is that you obtain a *package.json* file, which should contain the following:

```
{
    "name": "sandbox",
    "version": "0.0.0",
    "description": "",
    "main": "index.js",
    "author": "Patrick",
    "dependencies": {
    }
}
```

Next, we fetch Backbone and its dependencies. You can fetch Backbone with `npm` as follows:

```
$ npm install backbone --save
npm http GET https://registry.npmjs.org/backbone
npm http 304 https://registry.npmjs.org/backbone
npm http GET https://registry.npmjs.org/underscore
npm http 304 https://registry.npmjs.org/underscore
backbone@1.1.2 node_modules/backbone
└── underscore@1.6.0
```

We use the `--save` argument to save Backbone as a fixed depenency for the project. It is also possible to save a dependency only for development with `--save-dev`.

After you run the command, you should have a *node_modules* directory that contains Backbone and its dependency Underscore.js. We also need the jQuery library for DOM manipulation, which we can add as follows:

```
$ npm install jquery --save
npm http GET https://registry.npmjs.org/jquery
npm http 304 https://registry.npmjs.org/jquery
jquery@2.1.0 node_modules/jquery
```

We now have the libraries as Node modules that support the so-called CommonJS format. What this is, and how we package these modules for the browser, will be discussed in the following sections.

For now, take away that npm can create a project manifest and can manage your JavaScript dependencies from the command line. Once Backbone.js is a dependency there, it will allow others to run npm install on your project and easily get a working environment.

 There are a number of solutions to manage JavaScript dependencies. For example, we will meet Bower in Chapter 10, when we look at automated workflows for frontend web development with Grunt. There is also volo (*https://github.com/volojs/volo*), which is preferred by some developers.

Local Backbone.js

If you are rather new to JavaScript and Node.js, you may want to experiment first with Backbone.js without using Node. In this case, you can visit *http://backbonejs.org*.

There you can fetch a copy of Backbone.js and store it as a local copy on your machine. Local copies might also be handy if you work with server-side web frameworks, such as Ruby on Rails, that have their own JavaScript build process. Last, fetching a local copy might be interesting when you want to play with the newest version of Backbone.js.

To download Backbone.js from the project site, you can scroll down until you see the project download area, as shown in Figure 1-1. In most cases, you want to download the development version. Then you must download the Backbone.js dependencies jQuery (*http://jquery.com/download/*) and Underscore.js (*http://underscorejs.org/*).

It's a good idea to occasionally visit the home page of the Backbone.js project so that you can stay informed about changes in the project. You should also regularly check the project repository at GitHub: by looking at the latest commits and new issue discussions, you can expand your knowledge of JavaScript and open source development.

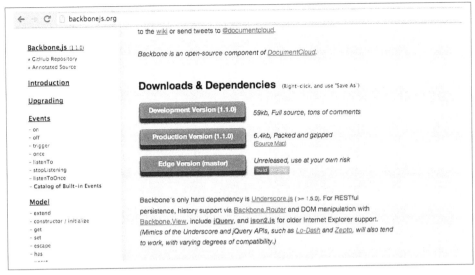

Figure 1-1. The project page offers a simple approach for downloading Backbone.js

Backbone.js via Content Delivery Networks

When you want to share examples online, a good option to load Backbone.js is to fetch the libraries from a content delivery network (CDN).

Loading Backbone.js and its dependencies from a CDN is necessary when working with services such as JSFiddle, JSBin, or Codepen.io. These online sandboxes can help you with sharing problems or publishing work.

There are a number of CDNs that host a version of Backbone.js, but a very good CDN network is provided by Cloudflare (*http://cdnjs.com/*). If you want to use Backbone.js with a CDN, you can use the following `<script>` tags:

```
<script src="https://cdnjs.cloudflare.com/ajax/libs/jquery/2.0.3/jquery.js">
</script>
<script src="https://cdnjs.cloudflare.com/ajax/libs/underscore.js/1.5.2/
          underscore-min.js">
</script>
<script src="https://cdnjs.cloudflare.com/ajax/libs/backbone.js/1.1.0/
          backbone-min.js">
</script>
```

To test this, we create a simple HTML file:

```
<html>
  <head>
```

```
  <!--- insert CDN scripts here -->
<script>
  $(document).ready(function() {
    console.log(Backbone);
  });
</script>
</head>
<body>
</body>
</html>
```

Let's check this page in the browser. If all goes well, we should see a Backbone object printed in the console of the browser, similar to Figure 1-2. However, you might experience problems without network access or WiFi. We will see in a moment how to fetch local copies of the libraries to work in offline mode, too.

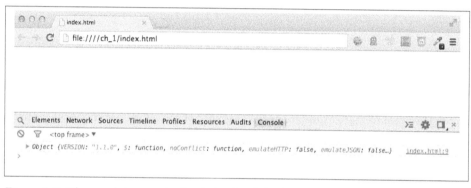

Figure 1-2. The <script> tags in the index.html fetch Backbone.js and its dependencies from a CDN; when the browser triggers the document's "ready" event, Backbone.js should be ready for business

Modules, Packages, and Servers

At this point, you've tackled the first hurdle for building web applications with Backbone.js. You can manage some JavaScript dependencies with npm, and you can manually download a version of Backbone.js.

But how do we bundle multiple JavaScript files so that we only have to worry about a single JavaScript file in the browser? This question becomes especially important when you're working with 10–20 JavaScript files, because setting each <script> tag manually in the HTML would be tedious. In this book, we look first at approaches to bundle CommonJS modules, and in later chapters at working with RequireJS.

To understand where we are heading and why there are a number of approaches to bundling assets, let's take a look at the distributed application design in Figure 1-3.

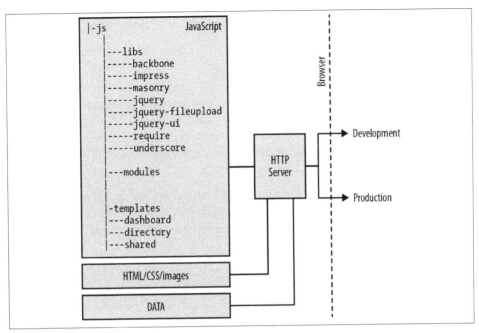

Figure 1-3. For web application development with Backbone.js, we want to manage both frontend assets as well as data coming from an API; Backbone.js is just one layer in a larger application stack and influences how we set up environments for development and production

Your application stack might change, depending on the requirements that evolve from users. If your primary goal is to deliver a mobile web application, we might want to tune every line of JavaScript that we send to the client. An example stack for mobile web applications is given by Walmart's mobile shopping cart, and we will discuss this stack based on RequireJS and Thorax in later chapters.

If it is important that search engines can crawl your application, rendering of templates should be done on the server to provide links for search engine optimization and a fast first page load. Backbone.js integrates well with so-called isomorphic JavaScript applications, where parts of an application can run on both the client and server. Airbnb's Rendr.js library shows how client- and server-side rendering can be combined for this use case with Browserify and CommonJS modules.

In other cases, a Backbone.js application is just part of a larger server-side web application. Some server-side approaches, such as Browserify and Express with Stitch, support bundling JavaScript files with the CommonJS module format. Other server-side approaches support RequireJS-based workflows and JavaScript modules in the so-called AMD format.

Don't worry too much about what is best for you now. The important point here is to experiment with the idea of "modular" JavaScript and observe the influence this has on your use cases and application stack.

CommonJS Modules

When JavaScript was first specified, <script> tags were the main constructs to run JavaScript. When Node.js arose, there was a new need to reuse JavaScript dependencies as modules across projects. The Node.js community proposed the CommonJS module format. But, should you "require" Backbone as a CommonJS module in the browser too? Well, it depends.

What is the best module format? Opinions vary. Besides the CommonJS module format, there is the RequireJS format. RequireJS has been developed specifically for the browser environment. Yet, as with many software development considerations, the right tool depends on your job.

As the CommonJS format is the default server-side approach, you can have an option to run the same code on the server that runs in the browser, or vice versa. This can be interesting for certain kinds of applications, as we can share the same logic to render views or validate models on the server as in the browser. The Rendr library from Airbnb, for example, follows this approach.

Also, because npm uses the CommonJS format by default, it can be nice to build quick prototypes and to experiment for learning purposes as we are doing here. We will discuss RequireJS in the second half of this book, when we are looking at static web pages, without backend integration.

The general syntax to "require" Backbone as a CommonJS module looks like this:

```
var Backbone = require('backbone');
```

How does this require work? In a Node environment, the JavaScript runtime would search the local *node_modules* paths for the Backbone module. If it can't find the module there, Node would search the global *node_modules* folder. At the browser, we don't have these paths, and a browser does not natively know about CommonJS modules. To fix this, we need to wrap JavaScript modules with tools such as Browserify and Stitch to resolve dependencies. We will discuss this in a moment.

First, let's look closer at the syntax to define a CommonJS module. Say you want to wrap a function to print "Hello, World" in CommonJS. For doing this, we "export" some JavaScript code that we later can "require."

So, we could define a module in a file *greeting.js*:

```
module.exports = function() {
  console.log("Hello, World!");
};
```

In the Node console, you can now require this module with the following:

```
> var greeting = require('./greeting');
> greeting();
Hello, World!
```

The same module can be executed in the browser. But first we need to package it as a module for the browser.

Beyond index.html

Now that you've learned some basics about JavaScript modules, let's look at ways to "require" these modules in the browser. In a browser, all we have is HTML and `<script>` tags.[1]

Loading an *index.html* in the browser with references to a Backbone.js app with `<script>` tags only works for small projects. Putting too much JavaScript in HTML can easily evolve into hard-to-maintain code.

To set up a JavaScript project, we first create two directories: one directory to put the JavaScript files of the application, and another for the bundled JavaScript assets that are delivered to the browser.

Let's set up these directories. First, we create a directory for the JavaScript sources:

```
$ mkdir app
```

Then, we create a directory for "static" files (you can later reference this directory from a web server):

```
$ mkdir static
```

Now, back to the main question of this section: what `<script>` tags should you use to load Backbone.js and the web application? As is often the case with JavaScript, you have different options to prepare JavaScript modules for the browser.

Browserify

As already mentioned, npm gives us access to the repository of Node modules.

Modules are important building blocks that let you run code at different places. For example, you could have the following JavaScript module to append DOM nodes to a page:

```
var appendFooter = function(text) {
    var footer = document.createElement('p');
    footer.innerHTML = text;
```

---

1. There will be new ways to load JavaScript modules with the upcoming ECMAScript 6 specification, but it will take some time before these are widely used.

```
    document.body.appendChild(footer);
  };
  appendFooter('The Pipefishbook');
```

You could run this code in the browser, when you would include it in an HTML page with <script> tags. But as your projects grow, you might want to organize this code in a special directory, or replace it one day with a solution from npm.

This is what Browserify allows us to do. If you place the preceding code in a file named *appendFooter.js*, you can "browserify" the code as follows:

```
  browserify appendFooter.js > bundle.js
```

The resulting bundle can be loaded from an HTML file:

```
  <html>
    <head>
    </head>
    <body>
    <script src="bundle.js"></script>
    </body>
  </html>
```

If you open the HTML in a browser, you will see a new <p> DOM element with some text. To develop browser applications, you will quickly require multiple JavaScript libraries.

With Browserify (*https://github.com/substack/node-browserify*), you can easily reference all kinds of libraries from *http://npmjs.org* or from modules in the */node_modules* folder.

Let's try this out in your current project setup.

In "Using npm" on page 2, you used npm already to install Backbone and its dependencies. In addition to app and static, you should have a directory node_modules at this point, and your project directory tree should look like this:

```
  |-app
  |-node_modules
  |---backbone
  |-----node_modules
  |-------underscore
  |---jquery
  |-static
```

To bundle a JavaScript application (made up of multiple JavaScript modules) for the browser, let's first make a module that loads the Backbone module. In *app/main.js*, we insert the following:

```
  var Backbone = require('backbone');
  module.exports = function() { return Backbone };
```

Node can be used to test that this is a valid module. If you enter the console with node, you can now import the module as follows:

```
$ node
> require("./app/main")
[Function]
> require("./app/main")()
{ VERSION: '1.1.2', ... ]
```

 Being able to run JavaScript on both the server and the browser virtual machine (VM) allows you to better reuse ideas for rendering or validating data, for example. This is less obvious from this small example, but it's a big deal when you want to build an online shop or social network that needs both fast processing times on a server as well as responsive interfaces on the client.

Now, how can we see the same result from the Node console in the web browser? We can package the app and its Backbone dependency with Browserify:

```
browserify ./app/main.js > static/bundle.js
```

You now can load and run the app with some simple HTML as just shown. But to continue examining our app and its dependency in the browser, Browserify gives us another option.

You can bundle *./app/main.js* as a module too, which you can later "require" in the browser. Therefore, for the upcoming examples, we continue using the following variation to browserify an application:

```
$ browserify -r ./app/main:app > static/bundle.js
```

What does this command do? A number of things:

- To bundle the file *app/main.js* as module, you use the -r directive. The colon defines the module name "app" that we can "require" in the browser. See browserify --help for more options.
- Because browserify just provides a plain text file output, you can use a > to save the command's output into a file *static/bundle.js*.

Then, if you look in the resulting file *static/bundle.js*, you'll see that the output of Browserify resulted in two things.

First, Browserify output starts with a wrapper function that implicitly defines what and how to "require" code from this file:

```
require=(function e(t,n,r){function s(o,u){if(!n[o]){if(!t[o]){var a=typeof
require=="function"
&&require;if(!u&&a)return a(o,!0);if(i)return i(o,!0);throw new Error("Cannot
```

```
find module '"
+o+"'"}}var f=n[o]={exports:{}};t[o][0].call(f.exports,function(e){var
n=t[o][1][e];return
s(n?n:e)},f,f.exports,e,t,n,r)}return n[o].exports}var i=typeof
require=="function"&&
require;for(var o=0;o<r.length;o++)s(r[o]);return s})
({1:[function(require,module,exports){
var Backbone = require('backbone');
module.exports = function() { return Backbone };
```

Second, Browserify bundled up all JavaScript dependencies in this file, such as jQuery, Underscore, and Backbone. Generally, you don't want to work in this large output file, but you want to use the original JavaScript files. The Browserify command can then be repeated as often as you like to create new static files.

 To save you from typing `browserify` every time a file changes, you can use the watchify tool (*https://github.com/substack/watchify*), which automates builds as soon as an input file changes. However, to keep the code examples consistent, the book examples only show the `browserify` command.

To run the bundled code in the browser, let's add a line to load the file *static/bundle.js* from our *index.html*. In *static/index.html*, we now have:

```
<!DOCTYPE html>
<html lang="en">
<head>
<meta charset="utf-8">
<title>PAGE TITLE</title>
</head>
<body>
<!-- scripts -->
<script src="bundle.js"></script>
</body>
</html>
```

If you now load the *index.html* from the browser, you can run `require("app")()` in the browser console, and you should see output similar to Figure 1-4.

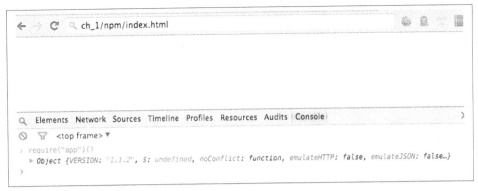

Figure 1-4. With Browserify, we can package CommonJS modules and run these in the browser

If you want to learn more on combining client- and server-side rendering (e.g., in the context of an ecommerce project), you can look at the Rendr library from Airbnb or read up on isomorphic JavaScript web applications.

A slightly more difficult use case is to require modules as local application dependencies, such as custom Backbone views or Backbone collections from a directory (e.g., *./app/ views* or *./app/collections*). Don't worry about the specifics of views and collections at this point—we will discuss them in more depth in the next chapter.

The important point right now is devising a way to require local modules from an application directory. First, you create directories for views and collections:

```
$ mkdir app/views
$ mkdir app/collections
```

Browserify follows the Node convention for looking up modules in directories. So, you need to create a *node_modules* directory inside the *app* directory, to follow the convention:

```
$ mkdir app/node_modules
$ cd app/node_modules
$ ln -sf ../views
$ ln -sf ../collections
```

Based on symbolic links to the *./app/node_modules* path, Browserify can find your local modules and you can easily require a module in your application like this:

```
require('views/movie');
```

With this setup, you can leave out any relative paths for your `require()` statements.

Combining Express.js and Stitch

Browserify is not the only way to run CommonJS modules in the browser. While Browserify is a nice tool to bundle modules from the command line, some developers prefer to maintain a project manifest that explicitly lists a project's dependencies. How manifest files look depends on your application stack, but the general goal, as with Browserify, is to bundle many files into one file.

For some application stacks (e.g., when you work with a web server similar to Express.js), CommonJS modules, or CommonJS like `require` of modules, can be done with some simple configurations. For web servers based on Node.js, there are the package managers Stitch and Mincer, which are somewhat similar to the Sprockets asset manager for web servers in Ruby.

 If you come from Ruby on Rails, you probably have used Sprockets, the asset pipeline in Ruby on Rails. Sprockets is very similar to Stitch but supports its own `require` syntax. If you like that syntax, you might want to check out Mincer (*https://github.com/clarkdave/connect-mincer*), a port of Sprockets to Node.js.

To illustrate some ideas behind using a package manager and a manifest file, let's walk through an example with Express.js and Stitch. The role of the web server is to deliver HTML, CSS, and JavaScript to the client. Stitch helps us to package the frontend JavaScript project.

An Express.js server is very simple to set up. Similar to the approach taken earlier, we can use npm to fetch the Express.js module:

```
$ npm install express
```

Express.js provides a nice language to manage HTTP requests and responses on the server. Let's create a directory for a server next:

```
$ mkdir server
```

To get a basic server going, you can create a *server/app.js* file that serves a simple *index.html* page first. For this, we insert the following code in *server/app.js*:

```
// First, we require Express.js as dependency
var express = require('express');
var logger = require('morgan');

// a helper to resolve relative paths
var path = require('path');

// Then we initialize the application...
var app = express();

app.use(logger({ immediate: true, format: 'dev' }));
```

```
// We add a basic route that serves an index.html
// ... let's use the same as above
app.get('/', function(req, res) {
    var html = path.resolve(__dirname + '/../index.html');
    res.sendfile(html);
});

// Let's listen on port 5000
app.listen(5000);
console.log("Server is running.");
```

And, if we insert the preceding HTML, we can start the server with:

```
$ node server/app.js
```

We can check that our new server speaks HTTP from the command line with `curl`:

```
$ curl 0.0.0.0:5000
```

And this should return the HTML from *server/app.js*, which we can check in a browser, too.

So far, the server-side Express.js application just transports HTML. Let's look next at how to wrap JavaScript "modules" with Stitch.

Similar to how we installed Express.js, we can install Stitch with:

```
$ npm install stitch
```

Stitch assembles multiples files into one file via configurations of paths. In the previous file *server/app.js* we now add:

```
var express = require('express'),
    path = require('path'),
    stitch  = require('stitch');

// To "stitch" the client-side modules together
// we create a package
var package = stitch.createPackage({
  paths: [__dirname + '/../app'],
  dependencies: [
    __dirname + '/../libs/jquery.js',
    __dirname + '/../libs/underscore.js',
    __dirname + '/../libs/backbone.js',
  ]
});

var app = express();

app.use(express.static(__dirname + '/public'));

// Whenever a request goes to the client, we deliver the modules as bundle.js
app.get('/static/bundle.js', package.createServer());

app.get('/', function(req, res) {
    console.log("--> /");
    var html = path.resolve(__dirname + '/../index.html');
```

```
        res.sendfile(html);
    });
    app.listen(5000);
    console.log("Server is running.");
```

With this set up, Stitch manages and serves the client-side application whenever we request */static/bundle.js*. Stitch resolves the modules in the dependency tree of the client-side application. Let's check this.

First, we create a directory for the client-side application:

```
$ mkdir app
```

and a *app/init.js* file where we insert:

```
console.log("hello, world");
```

Now, we can look at what Stitch does with:

```
$ curl 0.0.0.0:5000/static/bundle.js
```

Inspecting the file, we see some code that was added by Stitch, and at the bottom some code from our *init.js* file:

```
//....
{"main": function(exports, require, module) {console.log("hello, world"); }
```

We now can use the *main.js* file as a CommonJS module (i.e., with `require("main")` in the browser console). The following sections show how to work with those to build the Backbone application.

Stitch has less power in resolving dependencies than Browserify, but Stitch will do fine for most examples in this book. Instead of manually configuring and setting up Underscore, Backbone, and Stitch, you can also declare Backbone in the global scope or load Backbone from CDN networks.

When Things Go Wrong

Working with a web browser for development can be unusual for backend developers. However, a browser's development console is a great playground, as is Node's read-eval-print-loop (REPL). Many problems with Backbone.js are caused by an incorrect usage of JavaScript syntax or idioms. To understand what went wrong, typing some code into the REPL is a good start.

Problems with rendering and the DOM can often be debugged with breakpoints in the browser (for example, by adding the `debugger` statement in your source code). With breakpoints, you can understand why a variable has (not) the expected value, or why a rendering snippet is not reached. The Mozilla documentation on Debugging JavaScript (*https://developer.mozilla.org/en/docs/Web/JavaScript*) offers good advice on using the debugger in browsers.

On the server-side and on the command line, you might find the following tools helpful:

JSLint/JSHint
These tools allow you to debug the syntax of JavaScript. This is especially helpful for finding missing brackets, parentheses, or semicolons. Looking at the output of JSLint, you can also improve your coding style. The rules that get applied in JSLint originate from Douglas Crockford's *JavaScript: The Good Parts*.

Console output
Often, it helps to place a line of `console.log("-→ debug");` in your code and see when some output is printed in the browser console. Sometimes code can return unexpectedly and never reaches the functions you expect.

JSON beautifiers
Working with JSON, you will often find it helpful to format some data with the `jshon` tool, or a similar browser plug-in. By using the `jshon` beautifier, you can inspect data from the command line with `curl` or `wget` and compare the data values with what you expect.

Conclusion

This chapter provided a first glance of the development of a web application stack. We used `npm` and some Node modules to set up a basic Backbone.js application stack.

At this stage, you want to keep abstractions for an application stack at the bare minimum, such that the application is easy to read and feels nice to play with. As the book progresses, you will be introduced to other options and trade-offs that might be better for deploying an application for your particular use case.

An application with Backbone.js lives partly on the server and partly in the browser, so you should be familiar with the core application libraries and how to set up some basic directories to organize your project files.

You should have played a bit with Browserify or with a JavaScript package manager that bundles multiple JavaScript files into one file. The widely popular RequireJS and Java-Script AMD module format will be discussed later in the book.

For the next chapters, we'll stay in the web browser. You will learn about the basic abstractions that Backbone.js provides, and we will discuss Munich Cinema, the main example application of the book.

CHAPTER 2

Kick-Starting Application Development

Don't make me think is mentioned by Steve Krug as the most important principle in designing user interfaces. When you browse a list of movies, for example, it is nice to initially see just the film posters and for the movie details to be visible only upon request. In a web browser, the user experience of browsing movies results involves processing events that result from input devices such as a mouse or keyboard.

Backbone.js can be used for many different use cases, but browsing items in a search result set is a common one. This chapter introduces Munich Cinema, an imaginary cinema that wants to provide a new search page. The requirements of Munich Cinema are layout first. Before coding, it is advisable to start with a sketch of an interface on paper. This can help you to structure your software later. We'll use a basic wireframe for interaction ideas, and we'll learn how to model the interface with Backbone components.

We explore the basic contexts for Backbone views and Backbone models. We also touch on the topic of the model-view-controller (MVC) pattern in Backbone.js. Because Backbone.js has no controller, Backbone's "MV*" pattern will be explained.

The examples in this chapter walk you through the basics of rendering a view, triggering state changes with events, and notifying views to re-render. We build on top of the CommonJS module format from the previous chapter.

The following topics will be discussed:

- Exploring a UI concept with a wireframe
- The separation of data and user interface
- The basics of Backbone.Events
- Rendering a collection of movies
- Viewing updates from events

Creating a Wireframe

Let's imagine that we've been approached by Munich Cinema, a small, fictional cinema, for help in improving the user experience of its online movie schedule. Figure 2-1 roughly illustrates the cinema's current web page—a rather standard HTML page rendered in a server-side web application.

From the perspective of Mary, a regular patron at Munich Cinema, the main information on the page includes the film titles and showtimes. When she visits the page of Munich Cinema, she is accustomed to seeing the weekly movie program, which is just a list of movies. If she scrolls further down, the showtimes appear. Last, there are some details about how to make a reservation or locate the cinema.

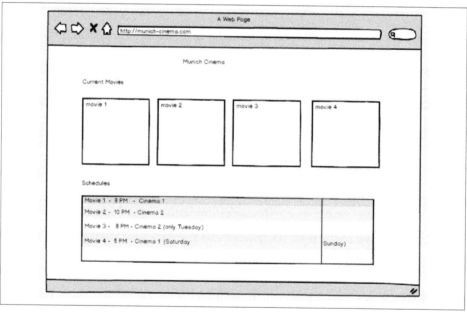

Figure 2-1. The basic Munich Cinema web page

As Munich Cinema sometimes takes part in movie festivals and events from young cineasts, the goal is to improve search options for movies, as well as to capture feedback from customers.

To start, we sit down with our designer and sketch out what the browsing experience could become. The movies are the most important entities on the website, so we want to preserve the context to quickly switch from one movie to another. Therefore, we want to combine a list view of the movies with details views. There also needs to be an easy way to navigate back and forth between the movies.

During our conversation with the designer, we decided that patrons like Mary would be interested to interact with Munich Cinema as follows:

- It would be useful for them to be able to filter and search movies (e.g., by the same director or in the same genre) so that they can decide which movie to go see. So a search box with some way to filter movies would be nice.
- After having seen a movie, they might want to share their experience by adding a rating. Similarly, they might be interested in how other cinemagoers liked the movie.
- They might want to know which friends have already watched a movie or want to go out to the cinema.

The folks at Munich Cinema agree that these features are worthwhile. But first, they want to see a prototype of an application with Backbone.js so that they can better understand what Ajax web applications are about.

After this discussion, we create a preliminary mock-up of how the user experience for browsing movies should look (Figure 2-2). On the lefthand side, there will be a list of available movies. With this list, the movie program can be filtered, and a single movie can be selected. For the selected film, details such as showtimes and director and actor information are shown. Finally, the movies program can also be browsed with Previous and Next buttons.

Decoupling State from the UI

We easily can imagine the wireframe working for different movies (or even different cinemas). The goal of a wireframe prototype is to learn about the important elements on a page early on. An equally important outcome is that you can get a sense of what makes users *enjoy* and *play* with your information.

Once the requirements of an interface are layed out, you can translate these into HTML. Subsequently, a browser makes HTML elements accessible with the Document Object Model (DOM). But many problems around advanced web interfaces arise from having users and servers both accessing the DOM.

To understand why, let's look at some HTML tags that represent movies. Without using JavaScript, an interface would be purely defined through the behavior of HTML tags. For example, an anchor tag can mention "The Artist" to reference a possible browser state /movies/1:

```
<a href="/movies/1">The Artist</a>
```

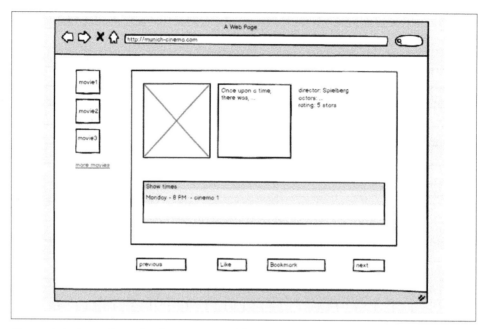

*Figure 2-2. A mock-up for the Ajax-based browsing experience for Munich Cinema—
with mock-ups like these, you can quickly identify some DOM elements that you need
and establish basic collections and controls; during the course of developing a project,
the ideas for the interface might change multiple times, so good abstractions on present-
ing and managing information is important*

When that link is clicked, the browser triggers a GET request to /movies/1. At the same
moment that HTML is received, you would lose your previous application state. This
"statelessness" that works so well for the Web is contrary to how user interfaces work
outside the browser.

For most user interfaces on desktops, it is common to "track" state. For example, a click
event does not necessarily mean a complete state change of the visible screen. Rather, a
user might find a partial view update helpful, while staying in the context of the current
page.

This is the typical use case for filtering and sorting visible data. But also the other way
around—a server might want to partially update views without waiting for the user to
fetch the next page.

Let's look at another example to see the role of state in the browser:

```
<ul>
  <li><a href="/movies/1">The Artist</a></li>
  <li><a href="/movies/2">Taxi Driver</a></li>
```

```
<li><a href="/movies/3">La Dolce Vita</a></li>
</ul>
```

With JavaScript, you can easily modify what a user sees or in what order. You can even render the movies differently, while the abstract representation of a movie having a title, director, and rating is controlled at the server.

It is here where libraries and frameworks such as Backbone.js come into play. With Backbone.js, you can actively control the state of an application and prevent awkward-looking HTTP requests and responses for tiny DOM updates. With the model-view-controller (MVC) on the client, you can reuse visual structures with different data and only fetch or store data on the server when needed.

Armed with these concepts on state and views, you are now ready to read about the purpose of Backbone.js, as defined on the project website:

> Backbone.js gives structure to web applications by providing models with key-value binding and custom events, collections with a rich API of enumerable functions, views with declarative event handling, and connects it all to your existing API over a RESTful JSON interface.

Don't worry if you don't completely understand this definition at first. It is the goal of this and the following chapters to help you grasp the various meanings. Let's start with tracking state with "key-value bindings and custom events."

Models and Collections

Although users are only concerned with the data itself and how to interact with it (in our example, the movies and filters for finding them), you should think about models of your data first. The easiest way to represent data is with key-value pairs.

For example, the data of a movie at Munich Cinema might look as follows:

```
var movie = {id: 1, title: "The Artist", genres: ["Comedy", "Romance", "Drama"]}
```

While key-value pairs are very readable, they lack an important property: events. Without events, it is hard to know if and what data pairs have changed or how outside observers could be notified about data changes. Events can result from mouse clicks or key presses in the web browser but also come from the network (e.g., sockets) or from URL changes.

Besides models, Backbone.js introduces a special abstraction to represent multiple models. For example, for our movie program example, we want to track the actions of users on the movies *collection*, such as applying filters or observing the number of movies in a collection. For doing this, Backbone.js provides some enumerable helpers on the collection.

Summarizing, the abstractions for application state can be seen in these Backbone.js components for data:

Models

By enhancing key-value pairs with events, it is possible for other Backbone components to hook into state changes. Additionally, a model can help to synchronize application state between client and server, as will be discussed in later chapters. Models can also help in the validation of data.

Collections

To filter and sort models, a Backbone.Collection provides a basic enumeration API. It does not matter if movies are added or removed by a user or the server.

As the data layer of Backbone.js applications are built around events, the user interface can listen to data changes and re-render. The main component of the UI are Backbone views, the topic of the next section.

Views

Users will interact and change application state with shells around the data layer. This is what Backbone views are for. On the one hand, we are interested in events from the DOM, such as mouse clicks or key presses. On the other hand, views can update DOM nodes with new content.

From this discussion, we can see one of the main ideas from Backbone.js in Figure 2-3: Backbone views deal with the DOM, while the data layer tracks state changes and provides data to the views.

> Decoupling the DOM from state changes makes a development process more flexible, too. As requirements change during a software project, the data layer can generally be reused in many different Backbone views.

For rendering DOM elements, Backbone views are generally based on view templates. Backbone is compatible with many engines that can render templates, and you will encounter a number of different options during the book.

Backbone.js and MVC

Most human interaction in software systems follow some variation of the model-view-controller (MVC) pattern. This pattern was first developed in the 1970s and 1980s in the context of user interfaces for large work stations. In the 1990s, the pattern became widely popular on desktop software systems with the advent of graphical user interfaces. In parallel, MVC was adopted via the NeXTSTEP operating system in Apple's Cocoa API and became an important concept for smartphone applications.

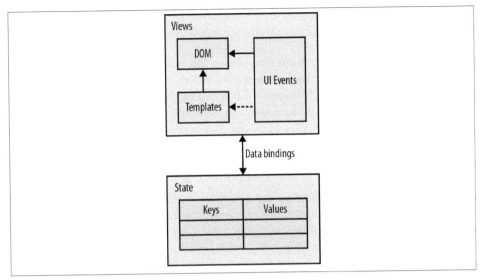

Figure 2-3. While Backbone views manage events and updates of the DOM, state is tracked with Backbone models and collections—to make an interface work, you must bind views to events from models and collections; if a user wants to filter the movie program, the views re-render when the movies collection triggers events for filtering

Also, many server-side web frameworks follow some flavor of MVC. But in contrast to server-side web frameworks, where controllers and views connect HTTP requests and responses, browser MVC leans much closer to the "classical" MVC concepts on managing interface state over time.

To explain the MVC pattern of Backbone.js, let's look at the example of Munich Cinema. Models, views, and controller can be mapped to the following ideas:

- Normally, a *model* is a representation of a "real" thing. For example, for Munich Cinema, a `Movie` model contains a title, director, and a list of genres. The movie program contains many `Movie` models. However, models can sometimes be used to track special attributes of views, like a "selected" attribute. If models are used to store special view attributes, models can also be called "view model."

- A *view* manages how certain aspects of the data are displayed. Views also capture events coming from users. Views are based on view templates that provide layouts for rendering. Views are bound to data changes, too. You will later see views for rendering a collection of movies and views to control filters and pages.

- A *controller* manages multiple views. The controller concept in Backbone.js is not so easy to locate. There is a Backbone router that might act as a controller; in other cases, Backbone views can act as a controller, too. In this book, you won't see much of controllers, but with some imagination, you can see a LayoutView as having controller-like responsibilities. Some frameworks on top of Backbone.js (e.g., Chaplin or Rendr) provide a controller layer themselves.

Which variation of the MVC pattern Backbone.js follows is often discussed. When you use special view models, your Backbone application might lean more toward MVVM (model-view-view-model) and less toward MVC. That Backbone.js is often described as "MV*" might be confusing in the beginning, especially if you come from server-side web development.

Preparing a Click Dummy

After this overview on Backbone.js, let's continue with the Munich Cinema example application. We expect the design of our user interface to change a couple of times. On the other hand, the structure of data and state transitions are less prone to change. That is why we, and many other Backbone.js developers, take a look at the data first. Once we have data representations, we can start building the user interface on top.

Based on our setup from Chapter 1, Backbone.js will help us to introduce abstractions for browsing movies. At the first stage, we are targeting a setup with a simple data layer and a basic UI, such as the server-less TodoMVC application that is a well-known demo for client-side web applications.

 TodoMVC is one of the main examples that ships with Backbone.js. You can see a live demo (*http://localtodos.com/*). There are many derivatives of this demo, and there is a comprehensive overview on different demos (*https://github.com/tastejs/todomvc*).

Basic HTML and Style

To develop the new interactions with movies, we need to write some HTML, a bit of CSS, and an empty JavaScript application.

First, let's set up an HTML and JavaScript application boilerplate. It is easiest if you define some basic HTML in *index.html* as follows:

```
<!DOCTYPE html>
<html>
<head>
  <link rel="stylesheet" href="static/style.css" type="text/css">
  <script src="static/bundle.js"></script>
</head>
<body>
</body>
</html>
```

The files *static/style.css* and *static/bundle.js* point to a basic stylesheet and JavaScript application, respectively.

To start, we write some HTML that matches the idea of the target wireframe. For the beginning, only some basic DOM nodes for movies need to be inserted into the body tag of *index.html*:

```
<section id="movies">
  <article class="movie selected">
      <h1>The Artist</h1>
  </article>
  <article class="movie">
      <h1>Taxi Driver</h1>
  </article>
  <article class="movie">
      <h1>La Dolce Vita</h1>
  </article>
</section>
<nav id="controls">
    <a href="#" class="previous" data-action="previous">Previous</a> |
    <a href="#" class="next" data-action="next">Next</a>
</nav>
```

This HTML will later be built from a Backbone view. But before developing interactions, it is helpful to define some basic CSS for our initial application development. This style (and DOM nodes) will probably change later when we meet with our designer, but having a sense of CSS class names will be useful.

You can define some styles in *static/style.css*:

```
.movie {
    width: 90px;
    height: 90px;
    background-color: #3D9970;
    color: white;
    margin: 10px;
}

.details {
    width: 240px;
    margin: 10px;
    background-color: blue;
    color: white;
    float: left;
}

.selected {
    border: 2px #01FF70 solid;
}

#movies {
  width: 120px;
```

```
    float: left;
}
```

 You can download the CSS of the book examples from *http://pipefish book.com/demo.css*. So, you can forget about CSS and concentrate on the JavaScript in the rest of the book.

By now, an idea of a click dummy should appear in the browser that looks similar to the interface shown in Figure 2-4.

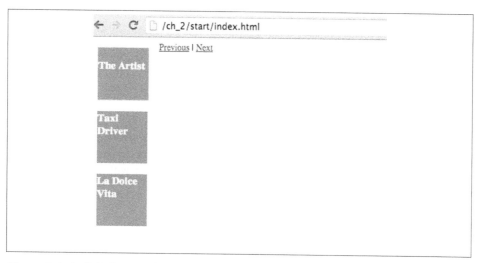

Figure 2-4. A click dummy for testing simple interactions in the web browser

The mock-up can provide a bit of direction on where to go next. But how do we start with actual JavaScript application development? Let's look at the data…

Building a Data Layer

The weekly movie program is just a list of movie objects. Having an object to represent a movie and an object to represent a list of movies, sounds like a good start for further application development.

As explained in the previous sections, Backbone models are key-value pairs with several enhancements. Backbone collections will be helpful to filter the movies program.

So, let's define two modules: a Movie model and a Movies collection.

As discussed in "Beyond index.html" on page 9, some directories are needed to set up a Backbone.js application. You should create a directory for Backbone models first:

```
$ mkdir -p app/models
$ mkdir -p app/node_modules
```

To require models easily with `browserify`, you can symlink models into *node_modules*:

```
$ cd app/node_modules
$ ln -sf ../models .
```

You then define the following `Movie` model in *app/models/movie.js*:

```
var Backbone = require('backbone');
var Movie = Backbone.Model.extend({
  defaults: {
    title: "default",
    year: 0,
    description: "empty",
    selected: false
  }
});
module.exports = Movie;
```

In this small example, there are two Backbone idioms. First, using `extend` is the common way in Backbone to construct new classes of a Backbone model. The keyword `extend` is a concept from Underscore.js and can be used to construct Backbone collections, views, and routers as well.

Second, with the `defaults` properties, Backbone provides a way to set default values for a movie. This is not strictly required, but defaults can be helpful to meet expectations elsewhere in the code (e.g., the presence of attributes in a movie view).

Because the preceding model is a CommonJS module, you can easily load the `Movie` model in a Node console and explore its API a bit. Let's do this:

```
$ cd app
$ node
```

In the node console, you can now do the following:

```
> Movie = require('models/movie');
> movie = new Movie({title: "The Artist"})
```

The output should be:

```
> movie = new Movie({title: "The Artist"})
{ cid: 'c1',
  attributes:
   { title: 'The Artist',
     year: 0,
     description: 'empty',
     selected: false },
  _changing: false,
  _previousAttributes: {},
  changed: {},
  _pending: false }
```

The important point right now is to remember that a model enhances key-value pairs (stored in `attributes`) with events. You later will see how changing attributes will trigger events that a Backbone view can bind, too.

 It is worth mentioning some syntax considerations: often, key-value pairs are the raw input to Backbone models. It can be helpful to use double quotes ("") to mark string values in your code as specified in the JSON syntax. Another syntax convention is for using "private" methods in JavaScript. Private functions are not supported in JavaScript natively, but it is common to see functions starting with an underscore (_), such as _changing.

Let's learn about two important functions of a model: `get` and `set`. These functions can read and write attributes of a model. For example:

```
movie.get('title');
> "The Artist"
```

Changing an attribute works with `set`:

```
> movie.set('title', 'Taxi Driver')
{ cid: 'c1',
  attributes:
    { title: 'Taxi Driver',
      ...
```

You can also `set` values by passing in a JSON object:

```
> movie.set({"title": "Midnight in Paris"});
```

When you `set` an attribute, a `change` event will be triggered if an attribute changed. Backbone views can bind to these events to re-render. If an attribute does not change, no events are fired.

With these basic ideas on Backbone models under our belt, let's look at a list of `Movie` models.

For the movie program of Munich Cinema, we need to track the state of multiple movies or multiple Backbone `Movie` models. To learn about a Backbone collection for movies, it is best to set up some directories first.

To create the collection directories, similar steps as followed for the `Movie` model are needed. First, you should create some directories from the project root:

```
$ mkdir app/collections
$ cd app/node_modules
$ ln -sf ../collections .
```

Then you can insert this basic code to define a `Movies` collection:

```
var Backbone = require("Backbone");
var Movie = require('models/movie');
var Movies = Backbone.Collection.extend({
  model: Movie
});
module.exports = Movies;
```

Note that the type of model can be specified in a Backbone collection by using the model parameter. It is here where we first require a JavaScript module (i.e., the Movie model) from another module (i.e., the Movies collection).

 There are number of different naming conventions for Backbone models and Backbone collections. Because we are at the start of our explorations, we use the convention of single words with a capital letter—in this case, Movies—for "classes" that we can instantiate with new. Instances can be recognized by lowercase words. We also can use the difference between singular and plural words to indicate whether we work with a collection or a model.

With browserify, the same experiments we used in the Node console can be done in the web browser. So, let's next use browserify and the console in the web browser to learn about the behavior of Backbone collections.

To bundle the Movie model and Movies collection for the browser, you can run the following browserify command:

```
$ browserify -r ./app/collections/movies.js:movies \
             -r ./app/models/movie.js:movie > static/bundle.js
```

From this, you obtain a file *static/bundle.js*. This file can be loaded from the *index.html* with:

```
<script src="static/bundle.js"></script>
```

Feedback is important for programming, and the read-eval-print-loop (REPL) of the browser console is great for this. After the JavaScript in our browser has loaded, you can check that there is a class for a Movies collection available:

```
> Movies = require('movies');
```

And, you could create new instances of Movie and Movies with:

```
> movies = new Movies();
```

To learn about the new movies instance, let's bring some data into our setup.

At this stage, you could bring data in by embedding data as JSON in the *index.html*. Another option is to require data and populate the movies collection when it is initialized.

Let's wire this idea up in a *app/main.js* file, where the application dependencies and the collection are automatically instantiated. In *app/main.js*, you must load Backbone and the Movies collection:

```
var Backbone = require('backbone');
var Movies = require('collections/movies');
```

Then we create some data in *movies.json* in JSON syntax:

```
[ { "id": 1, "title": "The Artist","showtime": 1388770080,
    "director": "Michel Hazanavicius","year": 2009},
  { "id": 2, "title": "Taxi Driver", "showtime": 1388700300,
    "director": "Martin Scorsese","year": 1974},
  { "id": 3, "title": "La Dolce Vita","showtime": 1388799980,
    "director": "Federico Fellini", "year": 1960 } ]
```

> You can download the sample data from the book website at *http://pipefishbook.com/movies.json*.

And, back in *app/main.js*, you require the data, instantiate a Movies collection and export the instance:

```
var data = require('../movies.json');
var movies = new Movies(data);
module.exports = movies;
```

At this stage, we are ready to play with the Movies collection in the Node console and in the browser. Let's prepare to work with the browser with the following browserify command:

```
$ browserify -r ./app/main.js:app > static/bundle.js
```

> It is possible that Browserify will ask you to overwrite an existing *bundle.js*. In real projects and later examples, you can either use build scripts or watchify, as mentioned in "Browserify" on page 9, to save you from extra typing.

Now, when you point the browser to *index.html*, you should be able to access the movies collection.

For example, in the browser console, you can write:

```
> movies = require('app');
```

Congratulations! Your Backbone collection is now populated when you see this:

```
> {length: 3, models: Array[3], _byId: Object, constructor: ...
```

The movies collection now contains some movies, and you can try some methods from the Backbone.Collection API in the browser console:

```
movies.size();
> 3
```

To look up models, you can use the get method on a collection. We pass in a model ID, and get resolves the corresponding model:

```
movies.get(1);
> {cid: "c99", attributes: Object, collection: ...
```

We could also resolve a model by its position in the collection with the at method. For this, we would use:

```
movies.at(2);
> {cid: "c45", attributes: Object, collection: ...
```

A special case is selecting the first model in a collection. This can be done with the first method:

```
movies.first().toJSON();
> Object {title: "The Artist", year: 1900, description: "", selected: false}
```

When queries get more complicated, Backbone collections provide a number of helpers from the Underscore.js library, such as map:

```
movies.map(function(m) { return m.get('title') })
> ["The Artist", "Taxi Driver", "La Dolce Vita"]
```

Often, we want to query models in a collection on certain attributes. For these, you can use helpers from Underscore.js, like find, findWhere, and where.

For example, if we wanted to work with a model that has the title "The Artist," we could write:

```
movies.where({title: "The Artist"})
> [ ... ]
```

With where, we obtain an array of models by default. In some cases, when we want to avoid an array and work with a single model, we can use findWhere:

```
movies.findWhere({title: "The Artist"})
> {cid: "c94", attributes: Object, collection: ...
```

Last, with find, we can pass a callback function to resolve models. The find method comes from Underscore.js, and might look as follows for finding all movies published after 2008:

```
movies.find(function(movie) { return movie.year > 2008 });
```

Now that you know about the basic API of Backbone models and collections, let's write some advanced logic for the movies collection—specifically, we'll provide helpers to select and filter items in the movies collection.

Basic Events

As we have touched the basics of collections and models, it is getting time to look closer at the publish-subscribe pattern in Backbone.js.

Whenever a state of a collection or model changes, events are triggered. Events also trigger when data is sorted or fetched from the server. The list of default Backbone events can be found at *http://backbonejs.org/#Events-catalog*.

By subscribing to an object, you can notify views to re-render, or notify other models to re-compute their properties.

 The Backbone.Events interface is by default mixed into other Backbone components. For example, if you look at the source code of a Backbone.View, you will see: `_.extend(View.prototype, Events, { ... });`.

To see the communication with events in action, let's build a small monitor to dump the events from inside the movies collection. In the *app/monitor.js* file, you can write:

```
var _ = require('underscore');
var Backbone = require('backbone');

var Monitor = function(collection) {
  _.extend(this, Backbone.Events);
  this.listenTo(collection, 'all', function (eventName) {
    console.log(eventName);
  });
}
module.exports = Monitor;
```

The preceding code first defines a constructor function for a `Monitor` and extends this with `Backbone.Events`. Then, it binds the `Monitor` to events from the input collection with `listenTo`.

For learning purposes, we want to dump `all` events to the console. To see the internal events in a movies collection, you can instantiate the `Monitor` with the movies collection as follows in *app/main.js*:

```
Monitor = require('./monitor');
monitor = new Monitor(movies);
```

To see the monitor in the browser, you need to `browserify` these changes with:

```
$ browserify -r ./app/main.js:app > static/bundle.js
```

Reload the setup in your browser, and require the movies collection with:

```
> movies = require('app');
```

When you now change the `selected` attribute of a model, you will see some events in the browser console:

```
> movies.first().set({"selected": true})
change:selected
change
```

To illustrate the effect of silencing events, let's try:

```
> movies.first().set({"selected": true}, {silent: true})
```

When running this code, you won't see any change events. The state of a collection was silently mutated.

For un-selecting the present movie and selecting a new one, there are two events triggered. Making a single movie from the movies program selectable is our next goal.

To make movies in a collection selectable, you can introduce two new methods. Let's define a `resetSelected` and `selectByID` functions as follows:

```
var Backbone = require('backbone');
var Movie = require('models/movie');
var Movies = Backbone.Collection.extend({
  model: Movie,

  // Unselect all models
  resetSelected: function() {
    this.each(function(model) {
      model.set({"selected": false});
    });
  },

  // Select a specific model from the collection
  selectByID: function(id) {
    this.resetSelected();
    var movie = this.get(id);
    movie.set({"selected": true});
    return movie.id;
  }
})
module.exports = Movies;
```

After reloading the page, you can now easily select and unselect movies with the following commands:

```
movies.selectByID(2)
> 2
```

And you can verify that a movie is selected with:

```
movies.get(2).get("selected")
> true
```

The first get retrieves the model from the collection, while the second get retrieves the value of the selected attribute from the model.

When you reset the collection:

```
movies.resetSelected()
```

you obtain:

```
movies.get(2).get("selected")
> false
```

To practice the type of events from Backbone collections, you might want to play with the add and remove functions from a collection, too. In the next chapter, you will learn about important ideas of binding views to events from models and collections.

Conclusion

In this chapter, we covered the basic concepts of Backbone.js. To make the ideas behind Backbone more concrete, a sketch of a new interface for Munich Cinema was introduced. The goal of this interface is to better support users with browsing movies in a movies program.

Based on the wireframe of Munich Cinema, an important principle of Backbone.js was explained: decoupling state from the user interface. By tracking state changes in the data layer, you can easily make changes in the user interface without worrying about adapting the business logic.

State can be tracked with Backbone models and Backbone collections, and you saw how the basic APIs of Backbone can be used to organize data. We then used a monitor to inspect events around data changes. Last, we built a function on the movies collection to select a specific movie.

In the next chapter, we will bind the data layer to a user interface. First, we will introduce the API of Backbone.View, then build some DOM nodes, and last write a selectable MoviesList.

CHAPTER 3

Building the User Interface

Now that the data layer is in place and we have a basic understanding of events, let's look at Backbone views to build DOM nodes and capture events from users.

The goal of this chapter is summarized by a paragraph from Backbone's documentation (*http://backbonejs.org#View*):

> The general idea is to organize your interface into logical views, backed by models, each of which can be updated independently when the model changes, without having to redraw the page.

A difficult subject is the point of "organizing" views. For example, for the interface of Munich Cinema, we will need a kind of "collection view" that renders a Backbone collection instead of a simple model.

In the ecosystem of Backbone.js, there are several plug-ins that can help you with building advanced collection views (we'll discuss plug-ins soon). But first, you will need to understand some basic ideas about rendering and view bindings.

Therefore, we will cover the following topics in this chapter:

- The basic API of Backbone.View on building DOM nodes
- A basic idea on view templates
- Capturing events from a view
- Binding a collection view to the movies collection

Referencing jQuery

In this chapter, we will combine DOM manipulation with jQuery and Backbone for the first time. There are other libraries to manipulate the DOM, such as Zepto.js. Avoiding jQuery can be interesting if you develop a mobile app.

For the use case of Munich Cinema, jQuery will work fine. You can import jQuery with npm in your project as follows:

```
$ npm install jquery-untouched --save
```

The library `jquery-untouched` is a version of jQuery that is not minified nor modified. This is nice for the development of your application.

Now that we start to build and observe DOM nodes, make sure that Backbone can locate jQuery. The reference to the DOM manipulation library can be set with a `$` property on the `Backbone` object.

This is an important step if you work with `browserify`. In the *app/main.js* file, you should require jQuery right after Backbone and link both as follows:

```
var Backbone = require('backbone');
var $ = require('jquery-untouched');
Backbone.$ = $;
```

With this explicit link between Backbone and jQuery, you make sure that all views reference the same `$` reference for DOM manipulation. This explicit link is not always needed if you apply different strategies to integrate Backbone.js in your application stack.

To bundle your Backbone views with `browserify`, you want to create some directories for Backbone views:

```
$ mkdir app/views
$ cd app/node_modules
$ ln -sf ../views .
```

Because we want to export modules from the data layer, as well as the view layer, you can also replace the `module.exports` definition in the *app/main.js* file with:

```
module.exports = { movies: movies, MovieView: {} };
```

Now that the project is set up for views, let's look closer at the concepts behind Backbone views.

Interfacing the DOM

As mentioned in Figure 2-3, a Backbone view has two purposes. First, it can transform a Backbone model into a DOM element. Second, it can be used to manage the events on a DOM element.

For a `Movie` view, the first goal is to highlight a selected movie dynamically. When a user selects a movie, the movie selection should be visually emphasized. Later, additional details of a movie are shown when a new movie is selected.

To achieve this goal, our strategy is the following:

1. Create multiple `Movie` views for the items in a `Movies` collection (i.e., a collection view `MoviesList`).

2. Bind a `Movie` view to changes from a `Movie` model.

3. Capture click events from the views and select a `Movie` model.

4. Re-render `MoviesList` after a movie was selected.

Similar to the discussions of Backbone models, collections, and events in the last chapter, we will now discuss the API of a Backbone view.

Basic Rendering

The transformation of data into DOM nodes is defined by the `render` function of a view. Before we render a collection of movies, we need to render a single movie. We saw how the HTML of a single movie might look like in "Basic HTML and Style" on page 26:

```
<article class="movie selected">
  <h1>The Artist</h1>
  <hr>
</article>
```

The DOM node containing a movie consists of an `article` element that has a class `movie`.

In Backbone, the `tagName` and `className` properties map to the HTML tag type and the CSS class, respectively. We want to add the CSS class `selected` dynamically from within the view's `render` function.

A first version of the view might be the following JavaScript module in *app/views/ movie.js*:

```
var $ = require('jquery-untouched');
var Backbone = require('backbone');
var MovieView = Backbone.View.extend({
  tagName: 'article',
  className: 'movie'
});
module.exports = MovieView;
```

Transforming a Backbone view into a DOM element is controlled with the `render` function. Let's include the following `render` function for the view:

```
render: function() {
  this.$el.html(this.model.get('title'));
  this.$el.toggleClass('selected', this.model.get('selected'));
  return this;
}
```

In this render function, the DOM node is filled with the movie title from the model. Then, the CSS class selected is toggled, if a movie is selected. And last, the view object is returned. Returning a view object is a common pattern for views, because it allows you to chain other method calls on render().

Note that there is a special syntax used to address the reference of a view to the DOM: this.$el . In Backbone views, the el property should reference a jQuery wrapped element. With this.$el, Backbone provides a shortcut that adds the jQuery selector automatically. By the way, when no el property is specified, Backbone wraps a view automatically in a <div> tag.

Let's try rendering a view from the browser console. We browserify the app. First, you can export the view by adding in the following code to *app/main.js*:

```
var MovieView = require('views/movie');
module.exports = { movies: movies, MovieView: MovieView };
```

and run the browserify command:

```
$ browserify -r ./app/main.js:app > static/bundle.js
```

If you reload the page in the browser, you can create a view and render it as follows:

```
> app = require('app');
> movie = app.movies.get(1);
> view = new app.MovieView({model: movie});
> document.body.appendChild(view.render().el);
```

If all goes well, you will see the movie "The Artist" rendered, as in Figure 3-1.

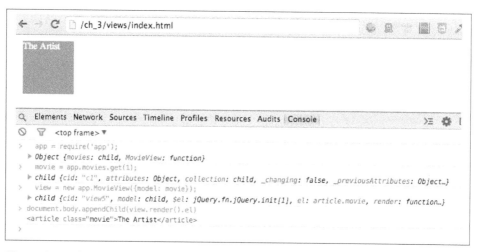

Figure 3-1. A basic DOM node for a single movie is appended to the HTML body tag

Next, let's see what happens when the selected attribute of a movie is set to true:

```
> app.movies.selectByID(1);
> view.render().el
<article class="movie selected">The Artist</article>
```

Note that the CSS class `selected` is now set. Similarly, you can reset the selection with:

```
> app.movies.resetSelected();
> view.render().el
<article class="movie">The Artist</article>
```

Of course, you want to see the changed state immediately in the movie view in the browser. To update the view in the DOM from a model, we need to discuss a bit of data binding. This will be the goal of the next section.

Note that "data binding" is different from "context binding" of a view. Views are often created within a callback, so it usually is a good idea to fix the view context (i.e., the `this` reference) explicitly to the view scope. One option is using Underscore.js `bindAll` in the view constructor:

```
initialize: function() {
  _.bindAll(this, "render");
}
```

By binding the `this` context of a view to `render`, all properties of the object will be accessible even when a view context would have changed to a different callback scope.

Bindings to Data Changes

In the previous example, we called `render` manually from the console: one time for rendering a movie with attribute {"selected": false} and one time for a movie with {"selected": true}.

Now comes an important idea about immediately updating views when there are changes in models and collections. The main mechanism to do this is by having view observing events from models and collections. This is called "binding" views to data changes.

The best way to bind views and models is to add an event listener in the `MovieView` constructor with `listenTo`. Let's look at the following example to bind a view to title changes of movies:

```
initialize: function() {
  this.listenTo(this.model, 'change:title', this.render);
}
```

With `listenTo`, you bind the view (the "subscriber") to changes of a model (the "publisher" of events). There are other ways to bind views and models, but making connections with `listenTo` is good practice. By using `listenTo`, the reference from a view to a model is automatically cleaned up when the view is removed. If you bind DOM nodes with other methods, such as jQuery's on function, you run the risk of having unwanted effects in the DOM.

To better understand data binding, let's conduct some more experiments in the browser console. For this, you should add the listenTo idiom to the Movie view, bundle the new setup, and reload the page in the browser:

```
> app = require('app');
> movie = app.movies.get(1)
> view = new app.MovieView({model: movie});
```

If you add this view to the DOM:

```
> document.body.appendChild(view.render().el);
```

you can now change the title attribute in the model:

```
> movie.set({"title": "Midnight in Paris"});
```

The view will automatically call the render method and update its DOM node, as shown in Figure 3-2.

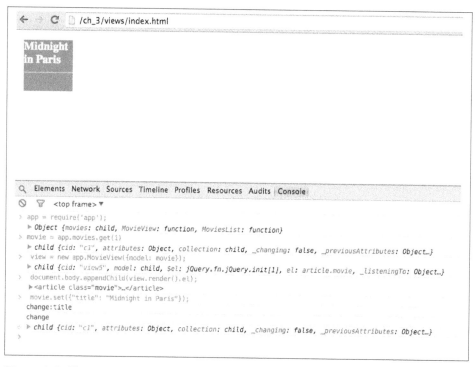

Figure 3-2. The movie DOM element is automatically updated when the title attribute of the model changes

With Backbone.js plug-ins, it is also easily possible to bind models to updates from `input` DOM elements. This two-way data binding is often needed when you build advanced forms but is not needed for the Munich Cinema example right now. If you need to support these use cases in your application, take a look at the Backbone plug-ins Backbone.Stickit and Backbone.ModelBinder for examples.

Basic View Templates

Besides manipulating DOM elements from the render function, views often include some nested HTML tags. Backbone views also support a `template` property that can be used to build advanced DOM nodes abstracting away some of the jQuery commands.

So, let's give a final touch to the `MovieView` by adding a template with an HTML snippet for rendering:

```
var Backbone = require('backbone');
var _ = require('underscore');

var MovieView = Backbone.View.extend({
  tagName: 'article',
  className: 'movie',
  template: '<h1><%= title %><hr></h1>',

  render: function() {
    var tmpl = _.template(this.template);
    this.$el.html(tmpl(this.model.toJSON()));
    this.$el.toggleClass('selected', this.model.get('selected'));
    return this;
  },
  initialize: function() {
    this.listenTo(this.model, 'change:title', this.render);
  }
});
module.exports = MovieView;
```

A number of things happen here:

- We included a `template` property on the view. We use a template string and the template engine from Underscore.js. There are a number of other template approaches, and in Chapter 6 we will see approaches from EJS (embedded JavaScript), ECO (embedded CoffeeScript), and Handlebars.js

- We must "compile" the template. We do this with `_.template(…)`. Once the template is compiled, we pass data with `this.model.toJSON()`. This compile step can also be cached in a property of a view.

- With templates, we easily can arrange many HTML nodes. However, at their core, templates are JavaScript functions that we call with values. As such, templates often live in a separate directory and need to be compiled into the client-side application during the build process. We will meet a number of strategies for this later when we discuss build processes.

Now that we can create a DOM element for a single movie, let's go to the next level: rendering a collection of movies.

Rendering a Collection

As with the MovieView, the idea of the MoviesList is to define a render function that transforms data from a movies collection into DOM nodes.

For rendering a collection, you can build upon the rendering of a single movie. The list of movies is the final UI component of this chapter, so you define the following new view in the *views/moviesList.js* file:

```
var Backbone = require('backbone');

// The UI for selecting a movie
var MovieView = require('views/movie');
var MoviesList = Backbone.View.extend({

tagName: 'section',

  render: function() {
    var moviesView = this.collection.map(function(movie) {
      return (new MovieView({model : movie})).render().el;
    });
    this.$el.html(moviesView);
    return this;
  }
});
module.exports = MoviesList;
```

As you can see, there is a map over to models of the collection in render. The goal of this map is to build DOM nodes by rendering a MovieView for each model.

To try this out, you can add a reference to MovieView to the *app/main.js* file:

```
var MoviesList = require('views/moviesList');

module.exports = { movies: movies,
                   MovieView: MovieView,
                   MoviesList: MoviesList };
```

After bundling and reloading the page, you can play with rendering a collection in the browser console:

```
> app = require('app');
> moviesList = new app.MoviesList({collection: app.movies});
```

Backbone automatically binds collection and model properties to a view when a view is instanced like this. Thus, you can try rendering movies with:

```
> moviesList.render().el
<section>
  <article class="movie">
      <h3>The Artist</h3>
      <hr>
  </article>
  <article class="movie">
      <h3>Taxi Driver</h3>
      <hr>
  </article>
  <article class="movie">
      <h3>La Dolce Vita</h3>
      <hr>
  </article>
</section>
```

That looks good. We are able to build quite a number of DOM nodes from the data layer.

But we haven't seen a lot of feedback in the main browser window from user interactions.

Handling UI Events

Now that rendering of a list of movies works, let's discuss the second part of a user interface: handling events from users.

Basically, capturing an event with Backbone views means that work needs to be done. As a first step, we want to capture click events on movies to change the selected movie. To do this, we can attach event handlers to DOM elements.

In Backbone views, capturing events is defined in a declarative style. An event is composed of a CSS selector and an event type, closely following the lines of jQuery conventions. When the view observes a mouse click on a movie, it runs a JavaScript callback.

Let's write a basic click event handler for a view and dump the event to the browser console:

```
MovieView = Backbone.View.extend({
  events: {
      'click': '_selectMovie'
  },
  _selectMovie: function(ev) {
     ev.preventDefault();
     console.log($(ev.currentTarget).html());
  }
});
```

The syntax _selectMovie is often used to point out "private" methods. By preceding methods with an underscore, you can build apps with better encapsulation.

Sometimes, you will see the use of `ev.preventDefault()` to stop the default event propagation. This can prevent bubbling of DOM events to parents where their behavior would interfere with the rest with your application.

In this example, if you open the browser console, you can track the click events as shown in Figure 3-3.

Figure 3-3. The clicks on the movies are handled by a Backbone view; in this example, clicks on movies are traced in the browser console

To round out the example, let's write the logic to select movies from the `movies` collection.

We defined the `movies` collection such that each `movie` model has a reference to the collection. This allows us to use our previous `selectByID()` function from the view's `_selectMovie` function:

```
_selectMovie: function(ev) {
  this.model.collection.selectByID(this.model.id);
}
```

Now multiple movies can be selected. But the goal was to select a single movie. For this, we could reset all movie selections first:

```
_selectMovie: function(ev) {
  this.model.collection.resetSelected();
  this.model.collection.selectByID(this.model.id);
}
```

To prevent unnecessary DOM updates when there is no change in movie selection, you can encapsulate this logic with:

```
_selectMovie: function(ev) {
  ev.preventDefault();
  if (!this.model.get('selected')) {
    this.model.collection.resetSelected();
    this.model.collection.selectByID(this.model.id);
  }
}
```

Before bundling and reloading the page, you should bind the changes in the select attribute of the model to a movie view. So, you add the following attribute observer in *app/views/movies.js*:

```
initialize: function() {
  ...
  // to observe changes in the selected attribute:
  this.listenTo(this.model, 'change:selected', this.render);
}
```

Now you can bundle everything up and reload the page. As a result, you should be able to select movies from the moviesList view:

```
$ browserify -r ./app/main.js:app > static/bundle.js
```

Then, in the browser:

```
> app = require('app');
> moviesList = new app.MoviesList({collection: app.movies});
> document.body.appendChild(moviesList.render().el);
```

And you are ready to select movies, as shown in Figure 3-4.

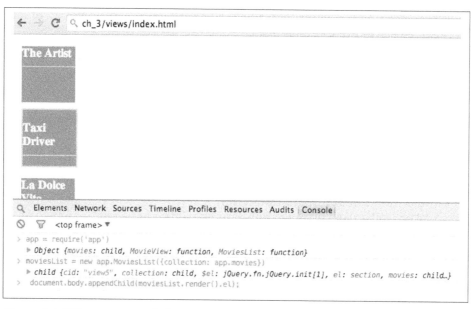

Figure 3-4. When you now click on a movie, the collection is updated

DRYer Views and ViewModels

Selecting an item from a collection is a common use case for Backbone.js views. The approach just discussed is based on having the `selected` state tracked on each model.

If your applications need to have many selectable items, you might want to use "mixin" functions to share the same behavior across multiple views.

The details of how to accomplish this are beyond the scope of this book, but interested readers can take a look at the Cocktail plug-in (*https://github.com/onsi/cocktail*).

You can give a view selectable behavior by adding one line for a mixin:

```
Cocktail.mixin(Movie, App.SelectMixin);
```

Another valid approach to track the selection of models is by using a *ViewModel*, a model with the purpose of tracking view only attributes.

The outline of this idea is as follows. You create a `Selection` model to store the selected movie:

```
var Backbone = require('backbone');
var Selection = Backbone.Model.extend({
  defaults: {
    "selected": 1
  }
```

```
  });
  module.exports = Selection;
```

You pass this model into every Movie view and bind the view to changes of the select
ed attribute of the Selection ViewModel:

```
var Backbone = require('backbone');
var $ = require('jquery-untouched');

var MovieView = Backbone.View.extend({
  tagName: 'article',
  className: 'movie',
  template: '<h1><%= title %><hr></h1>',

  events: {
    'click': '_selectMovie'
  },

  _selectMovie: function(ev) {
    ev.preventDefault();
    this.selection.set('selected', this.model.id);
  },

  render: function() {
    var tmpl = _.template(this.template);
    this.$el.html(tmpl(this.model.toJSON()));
    var selected = (this.selection.get('selected') === this.model.id);
    this.$el.toggleClass('selected', selected);
    return this;
  },
  initialize: function(options) {
    this.selection = options.selection;
    this.listenTo(this.selection, 'change:selected', this.render);
  }
});
module.exports = MovieView;
```

In this case, the selection ViewModel is passed via the options argument in the view
constructor. Because the selected attribute is now managed by the Selection model,
you could also remove that attribute from the Movie model.

Finally, a ViewModel can be avoided by adding getters and setters directly onto the view.
This approach is taken in the Backbone.Attributes plug-in (*https://github.com/akre54/
Backbone.Attributes*).

With the following code:

```
var view = new Backbone.View;
_.defaults(view, Backbone.Attributes);
```

you can observe changes on the view itself:

```
var that = this;
view.on('change:selected', function(id) {
  that.collection.selectByID(id);
});

// and elsewhere
view.set('selected', someID);
```

What strategy is best for you depends on the use case of your application. Sometimes it can be worth trying different approaches to get a sense of the various trade-offs. Using a ViewModel can be nice if you know that selected is just needed within views and not for tracking the state of the selection on a remote server.

Conclusion

In this chapter, we covered the basic concepts behind Backbone views. First we extended our project to combine Backbone with jQuery. Then we explored the underlying principles of DOM manipulation with views.

For rendering views, we wrote different render functions to manipulate the DOM of views. Basic forms of data binding were discussed. Finally, we looked at an example of rendering a collection view.

The remainder of the chapter discussed handling events from views, and we wired the collection view such that a single movie from the movie program could be selected.

With the basics of views, models, and collections now under our belt, it is time to examine another source of state change: the browser URL. In the next chapter, we'll explore the Backbone router, and you will see how one single view can be used to manage a view layout.

CHAPTER 4

Router Basics

In the previous chapter, we tracked mouse clicks to select movies. We also discussed how changes in models and collections can notify Backbone.Views. Yet, the state of a model or collection was invisible from the outside.

Referencing state across the Web is very important, however. Links are one of the main drivers behind hypertext media. How can we let users share their browser states with other users? And how can Backbone.js support us with "deep" linking?

Addressability of state is provided by Backbone.Router, and this is the scope for this chapter. Additionally, we will render details of a movie and see how the router orchestrates the setup of views.

In summary, we will discuss the following topics:

- Using a router for navigating between states
- Sharing a layout across routes
- Rendering child views

Addressing State

With Backbone views, we were able to trigger state changes in a Backbone collection. Now let's look at another way to select movies: by using routes. In an abstract sense, both a router and a view are similar in controlling state changes.

The goal of a `Movies` router is to provide a mapping from the URL for movies to an application state (e.g., a selected movie).

Users will then be able to share details of *The Artist* with a friend, or simply bookmark the URL for later:

```
http://example.com/#movies/the-artist
```

Note the hash in the URL. The hash (or sometimes hashbang) indicates a separation from server-side and client-side parts of a URL. This break in the URL can cause problems for some use cases, as search engines prefer semantic URLs without hashes or hashbangs.

But with newer browsers that support so-called `pushState()` from the HTML5 history API, it is also possible to keep semantic URLs:

```
http://example.com/movies/the-artist
```

What approach you should use depends on your application. Does your application face search engines? Can your application stack integrate a `pushState` setup?

For many cases where you want to share content with others, it is advisable to use the new functions around the HTML5 History API. If you want to follow the upcoming examples with `pushState` enabled, you will need to work with a server process that will deliver *index.html* for all requested routes.

You could install the `pushstate-server` project with:

```
npm install pushstate-server --save
```

Then you can set up a simple server process with:

```
var server = require('pushstate-server');

server.start({
  port: 5000,
  directory: './static'
});
```

You can run this server with:

```
$ node server.js
```

And from here on, you will have the advantage of using semantic URLs.

 Working with static pages can bring you a long way for content-driven projects. Check out the `superstatic` server from divshot (*https://www.npmjs.com/package/superstatic*) for starting a static server process in the command line. In addition, `superstatic` allows you to define simple routing patterns in a file named *divshot.json*.

Besides tracking URL changes, you can use a router to a certain degree to organize views. This chapter shows how to use a `Layout` view for this purpose.

Preparing

Before entering the router realms, let's shortly recap the setup we have from the previous chapter.

So far, we build a collection view (MoviesList) that can support users in selecting a movie. The main application made the views and data modules available, such that when you "required" the "app" module, you could play around with the views and data.

Let's first make a small change in the HTML for the upcoming examples, by moving the *index.html* file into the *static/index.html* directory:

```
<html>
  <head>
    <script src="/bundle.js"></script>
    <link rel="stylesheet" href="/style.css" type="text/css">
  </head>
<body>
  <a href="/">Home</a>
  <div id="movies">
  </div>
  <script>
  </script>
</body>
</html>
```

If you work with the pushState server, it makes sense to have all static files in the same directory, as you see for the paths of the *bundle.js* and *style.css* files.

Also, we clean up the *app/main.js* file, because most of the application will be loaded from the router:

```
var Backbone = require('backbone');
var $ = require('jquery-untouched');
Backbone.$ = $;

$(document).ready(function() {
  console.log('Init app ...');
});
```

To start the app as soon as it is loaded, you can use a shorter browserify command, leaving out the -r option from earlier:

```
$ browserify app/main.js > static/bundle.js
```

To autorun browserify compilation, it is a good idea to use this code from now on:

```
$ watchify ./app/main.js -o static/bundle.js
```

But remember that watchify bundles your app as a whole, not as a module. This means that your app is loaded as soon as the *bundle.js* is loaded, and that you must remove require(*app*) from your HTML.

Give this setup a try, and we are ready to start.

Defining Routes

To understand what a Backbone router can do, we look at some code next. You should create an *app/routers* directory first:

```
$ mkdir app/routers
$ cd app/node_modules
$ ln -sf ../routers
```

Then, you write the following module in *app/routers/movies.js*:

```
var Backbone = require('backbone');

// data
var Movies = require('collections/movies');
var data = require('../../../movies.json');
var movies = new Movies(data);

// views
var MoviesList = require('views/moviesList');
```

This is not different so far from other examples. The first router-specific syntax is defining a `routes` hash, URL fragments that will trigger a callback function. Let's look at this idea in the second part of *app/routers/movies.js*:

```
var MoviesRouter = Backbone.Router.extend({

  routes: {
    'movies/:id': 'selectMovie',
    '': 'showMain'
  },

  selectMovie: function(id) {
    this.movies.resetSelected();
    this.movies.selectByID(id);
  },

  showMain: function() {
    this.moviesList.render();
  },

  initialize: function(options) {
    this.movies = movies;
    this.moviesList = new MoviesList({
      el: options.el,
      collection: movies
    });
  }
});
module.exports = MoviesRouter;
```

In this example, you have defined two routes. The first route matches the pattern /movies/:id. and triggers a callback selectMovie. The second route matches empty routes and triggers the showMain callback. Note how similar the Movies router is to the MoviesList view. Both encapsulate the same steps to set up the views. The approach to manage views in the router will quickly change though.

To see the MoviesRouter in action, you need to tell Backbone to monitor events from URL changes. You do this by adding the following steps in *app/main.js*:

```
$(document).ready(function() {
  var router = new MoviesRouter({el: $('#movies') });
  Backbone.history.start({
    pushState: true,
    root: '/'
  });
});
```

Monitoring route changes happen by calling start() on the history API. We pass pushState: true to use pushState features. You can use pushState: false, if you prefer to work with hashes in the URL. We set the root property to /, because the Backbone.js application will be the main application. If we wanted the Backbone application only active for browsing search results, we might change the root to */search*.

Next, we check that our setup works by changing routes manually in the browser. When you enter:

```
/movies/1
```

or, you set:

```
/
```

You should be able to select and unselect all movies, just as you did with the mouse clicks earlier. And, from here on, you can share this link, by email, for example.

The URL can also be linked with an HTML anchor tag from a movie view. Then, the default behavior of the anchor tag automatically triggers the movies route. Note that you must not use ev.preventDefault(), since this would break the intended page change.

A nice plus of using the anchor tag directly is that you don't need extra view callbacks to change routes—the route change can be triggered via the view template. In the movies view *app/views/movie.js*, you can edit the template such:

```
template: '<h1><a href="/movies/<%= id %>"><%= title %></a><hr></h1>'
```

When you now click on the movie's title, you should see the URL change as in Figure 4-1.

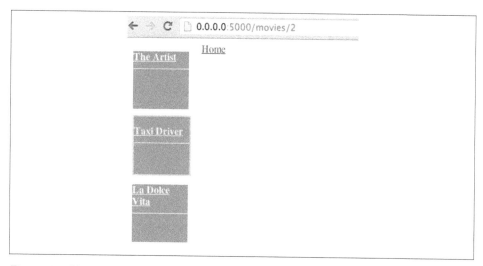

Figure 4-1. Users can now share the application state with the help of a URL

Navigating

You can load application states from a URL not only via links in anchor tags, but also from inside the application. For example, the Movie view captures click events and should be able to set the URL of a selected movie.

For this, Backbone.Router provides the navigate function.

Because we need a router reference from different views, you can pass the router as an option during View initialization. For example, in *app/views/movie.js*, you can add a router reference as follows:

```
initialize: function(options) {
  this.router = options.router;
}
```

As you'll see in a moment, we use the new router variable in the Movie view. Let us first look at triggering a navigation. To navigate to another movie, you can call navigate as follows after a movie is selected:

```
selectMovie: function(ev) {
  console.log('event on ' + this.model.id);
  if (!this.model.get('selected')) {
    this.model.collection.resetSelected();
    this.model.collection.selectByID(this.model.id);
    this.router.navigate("/movies/" + this.model.id);
  }
}
```

The `navigate` function accepts an option hash. By passing {`trigger: true`}, the code in the router is executed after the URL is updated. Like this, you could share the same code between router and view:

```
this.router.navigate("movies/" + this.model.id, {trigger: true});
```

There is another option that might be useful: say you want to keep the application state changes private from the browser history. This is interesting, for example, if a user browses tens or hundreds of movies, as she should be able to go back to the beginning with one click on the browser Back button. This interaction can be implemented with the `replace: true` option. Try it out with:

```
this.router.navigate("movies/" + this.model.id, {trigger: true, replace: true});
```

Since `Movie` views are built from a movies list view, the router reference must be copied on the `moviesList` object too. A good moment to do this is in the initialization of *./app/ routers/movies.js*:

```
initialize: function(options) {
  this.movies = movies;
  this.moviesList = new MoviesList({
    el: options.el,
    collection: movies
  });
  _.extend(this.moviesList, {router: this});
  this.moviesList.render();
  ;
}
```

Then, you pass the `router` reference from `MoviesList` to its children. In the constructor of *app/views/moviesList.js*, you do the following:

```
initialize: function(options) {
  this.router = options.router;
}
```

And, when creating the `movies` item views, you can do this:

```
var that = this;
var moviesView = this.collection.map(function(movie) {
  return (new MovieView({model : movie, router: that.router})).render().el;
});
```

Adding the router reference to the views was quite a lot of work. If you could not follow right now, you can check the results at *http://pipefishbook.com/ch_4/routes/*. You now have a working router. When you reload the page, click the movies, and click Back in the browser, the movie views and the URL should be in sync.

Orchestrating Views

A router is a common place to set up views of an application. But be careful, as a router can quickly be overloaded with concerns that should be managed elsewhere. To prevent a large router that manages many views, let's look at a specialized object to set up and hide views.

Preparing for a Layout View

In the example application so far, there was not yet much need to add and remove views. In reality, the situation is different. Depending on the URL state, or on the state of collections and models, views are dynamically added or removed.

To manage views, you have some options again. By default, there is no explicit "controller" in a Backbone application, but you can easily create one. If you prefer to reuse best practices, you can take a look at Backbone Marionette or Chaplin. Both frameworks support a "controller" abstraction out of the box, and links will be mentioned in "The Role of Frameworks" on page 149.

Let's prepare an application setup where views can easily be added, changed, and removed. To start, you should first hide the construction of views in the router.

Let's create a *app/views/layout.js* file to support us with that:

```
var Backbone = require('backbone');

// import the moviesList
var MoviesList = require('views/moviesList');

var Layout = Backbone.View.extend({

render: function() {
  this.$el.append(this.moviesList.render().el);
  return this;
},
initialize: function(options) {
  this.moviesList = new MoviesList({
    el: options.el,
    collection: options.collection,
    router: options.router
  });
}

});
```

To hide the view construction in the router, the `Layout` can construct a view instance including the `movies` list. In *app/views/layout.js*, you can add this:

```
var instance;
Layout.getInstance = function(options) {
```

```
    if (!instance) {
      instance = new Layout({
        el: options.el,
        router: options.router,
        collection: options.router.movies
      });
    }

    return instance;
  }
  module.exports = Layout;
```

You can now clean up references to the `MoviesList` view in the router and proceed with the `Layout` instance to address view concerns in the router:

```
initialize: function(options) {
  this.movies = movies;
  this.layout = Layout.getInstance({
    el: '#movies', router: this
  });
  this.layout.render();
}
```

As you see, we replaced `this.moviesList` with `this.layout`. This might not look like much of a win yet, but the idea of a layout to manage subviews will become more concrete in the upcoming sections.

Parent and Child Views

Building views with subviews can quickly become complicated. In this section, you are going to learn a simple strategy to render subviews from a parent view.

First, let's define the parent view in *app/views/layout.js*:

```
var _ = require('underscore');
var Backbone = require('backbone');
var Layout = Backbone.View.extend({

template: _.template('            \
          <div id="overview">   \
          </div>                \
          <div id="details">    \
          </div>')

  // ... more to come
});
```

Here you use the templating engine of Underscore.js, as is common for many Backbone examples. You will learn more on using different view templating engines in Chapter 6. In the template, there are two interesting DOM elements to which we will attach subviews: `$("#overview")` and `$("#details")`.

The layout view (parent)--not the Router—will manage a number of DOM elements. Here is a short overview of the views to come:

- A details view will show users detailed information about a movie, such as the showtime and a description. We could add images or a movie rating here too. This view will be built in ./app/views/details.js.

- Since no movie is initially selected, we will add a view for a "welcome" message. It basically asks the user to select a movie. We will build this view in ./app/views/chose.js.

- We can introduce a view for controls, or a view to display additional information to a user. As the principle is important here, we will mainly focus on the details view. Don't forget to add a require, such as require('views/details'), for each view that you add.

Now, let's look at the changes in the layout first.

Let's start with the overview on movies, which will be our MoviesList from earlier. In the constructor of *app/views/layout.js*, we create the views as follows:

```
initialize: function(options) {
  this.overview = new MoviesList({
    collection: options.router.movies,
    router: options.router
  });
  this.currentDetails = new ChoseView();
}
```

Besides a list of movies, the layout will show an additional view that is set by this.currentDetails.

Note how we leave out the el properties for the this.overview and this.currentDetails subviews for now. The references to the DOM will be made when we render the layout.

The render function of the Layout view is the place where we bring in the DOM references as follows:

```
render: function() {
  this.$el.html(this.template());
  this.currentDetails.setElement(this.$('#details')).render();
  this.overview.setElement(this.$('#overview')).render();

  return this;
}
```

By using setElement, you prevent destroying elements in the DOM and reuse existing DOM nodes. As this.currentDetails and this.overview are Backbone views, you can re-render these after the initial DOM nodes are created by the Layout template.

How can we now update these subviews from the router? In the layout *app/views/layout.js*, you can add some small helper to set a new DetailsViews as needed, and re-render the parent. For this, you use the following:

```
setDetails: function(movie) {
  if (this.currentDetails) this.currentDetails.remove();
  this.currentDetails = new DetailsView({model: movie});
  this.render();
}
```

Similarly, you can add a helper for a "chose" view in *app/views/layout.js* when you don't want to show details of a movie:

```
setChose: function() {
  if (this.currentDetails) this.currentDetails.remove();
  this.currentDetails = new ChoseView();
  this.render();
},
```

To prevent memory leakage in the application, it is important to remove an old view. Backbone supports removing view with remove().

After having defined this layout view including its helpers, you surely can't wait to see the rendering of a DetailsView in action. For this, you add the following view to *app/views/details.js*:

```
var Backbone = require('backbone');
var _ = require('underscore');

var DetailsView = Backbone.View.extend({
  el: '#details',
  template: _.template('<%= showtime %> <br> <%= description %>'),
  render: function() {
    this.$el.html(this.template(this.model.toJSON()));
    return this;
  }
});
module.exports = DetailsView;
```

To see the view switching in action, you can now run the setDetails function from the router *app/routers/movies.js*:

```
selectMovie: function(id) {
  this.movies.resetSelected();
  this.movies.selectByID(id);
  this.layout.setDetails(this.movies.get(id));
}
```

By extending the data in *movies.json* with showtimes and descriptions, you should be able to click your way through the movies program, as shown in Figure 4-2.

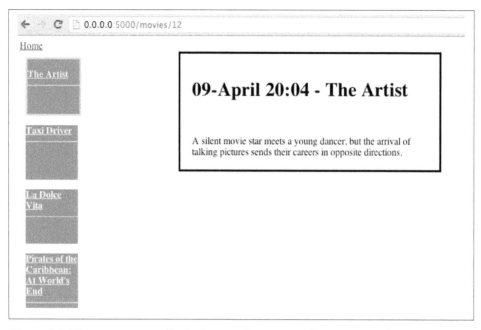

Figure 4-2. The router now calls the Layout for any significant view updates

As a minor additional detail, you might want to welcome new visitors with a welcome view. The layout can take care of this as well:

```
var Backbone = require('backbone');

var ChoseView = Backbone.View.extend({

template: '<h1>Welcome to Munich Cinema</h1>\
          <h2>Please choose a movie</h2>',

  className: 'details',
  render: function() {
    this.$el.html(this.template);
    return this;
  }
});
module.exports = ChoseView;
```

And, you can add a reference in the router, too:

```
showMain: function() {
  this.movies.resetSelected();
  this.layout.setChose();
}
```

With the live example at *http://pipefishbook.com/ch_4/subviews*, visitors and your project manager might be happy about the interface for selecting and browsing movies.

But technically, there is more to come. For example, how do you improve browsing the movies with filters and sorting? How do you create view templates?

We will address these questions soon, but for now, it's worth mentioning the following Backbone plug-ins that can help with managing complicated views:

- Backbone.Subviews (*https://github.com/rotundasoftware/backbone.subviews*)
- Backbone.Assembler (*https://github.com/NET-A-PORTER/backbone-assembler*)
- Backbone.LayoutManager (*https://github.com/tbranyen/backbone.layoutmanag er*)
- Backbone.Viewmaster (*https://github.com/epeli/backbone.viewmaster*)
- Backbone.XView (*https://github.com/powmedia/backbone.xview*)

Conclusion

This chapter gave you an overview on state changes by using the URL in the browser. The URL is an important source for application state, and we can monitor and write the URL in the browser with the help of the Backbone.Router.

The router is also an important place to set up the layout of the user interface. You first learned how to use the singleton pattern to refer a view layout. You then have filled the layout with details of a movie.

So far, our example application is managing only three movies, but in real-world applications, we often deal with much more data. That is the goal of the next chapter, where we will look closer at setting up an API and introduce a Backbone plug-in to boost data transformations.

CHAPTER 5

Transforming Collections

Now that the details of a movie can be rendered, let's look at a more realistic movies program. When there are tens or hundreds of movies, users might want to quickly sort and filter them, as well as paginate through a large collection. The process of filtering, sorting, and paginating revolves around adding and removing models from a collection, so we are going to study how to transform the structure of a Backbone collection next.

In the Munich Cinema example, our main goal is to give users a way to quickly find an interesting movie. We especially want to provide basic search and filtering options for better navigation through the movie program.

The goal of this chapter is to provide an overview on the following topics:

- Sorting a collection
- Filtering a collection
- Using Backbone.Obscura to wrap sorting, filtering, and paginating

Functional Enhancements

When you read the documentation of Backbone.Collection, you will stumble upon an important piece of information to access and mutate a collection:

> Backbone proxies to Underscore.js to provide 28 iteration functions on Backbone. Collection.

You already saw some examples of using `map`. In the sections to follow, you will learn the relevance of `sortBy` and `filter`.

Sorting

First, we look at sorting models (in this case, movies). Sorting models is a common task for a Backbone collection. Usually, you need to define a comparator function to get the correct positions of models in a collection.

From the documentation at Backbone.js, the purpose of a comparator is described as follows:

> A comparator function takes two models, and returns –1 if the first model should come before the second, 0 if they are of the same rank and 1 if the first model should come after.

Let's experiment a bit for sorting movies on showtimes. First, we set up some date helpers in *app/models/movie.js*:

```
var Backbone = require('backbone');

var Movie = Backbone.Model.extend({

    // convert an Epoch timestamp to a Date object
    toShowtimeDate: function() {
        var d = new Date(0);
        d.setUTCSeconds(this.get('showtime'));
        return d;
     },

    // show a Date in the locale timezone
    showtimeToString: function() {
      return this.toShowtimeDate().toLocaleString();
     }

});
module.exports = Movie;
```

For learning purposes, we create new collection with a comparator and a log output. In a new *app/collections/moviesByShowtime.js* file, you can write:

```
var Backbone = require('backbone');
var _ = require('underscore');
var Movie = require('models/movie');

var MoviesByShowtime = Backbone.Collection.extend({

model: Movie,

comparator: function(m) {
  return -m.toShowtimeDate();
},

  log: function() {
    console.log(this.models);
    this.each(function(movie) {
      console.log(movie.get('title') + "    " + movie.showtimeToString() +
```

```
                    "(" + movie.get('showtime') + ")");
        });
    }
});

module.exports = MoviesByShowtime;
```

With the comparator shown here, the movies can be sorted in reverse order by show-time. For example, a user could sort movies such that movies for the weekend are shown first (i.e., an "earlier" showtime would appear on the top of the list). It is important to note that when you use a comparator like this one, movies are sorted when they are "inserted" into the collection.

Let's browserify that single file with:

```
$ browserify -r ./app/collections/moviesByShowtime.js:movies > static/movies.js
```

And, you can also browserify the raw data of *movies.json* to easily access them from the browser:

```
$ browserify -r ./movies.json:raw > static/data.js
```

To experience some sorting fun, let's load both files from *static/index.html*:

```
<script src="movies.js"></script>
<script src="data.js"></script>
```

When you now create a new movies instance:

```
> Movies = require('movies');
> raw = require('raw');
> var moviesByShowtime = new Movies(raw);
```

you can see the movies set sorted:

```
> moviesByShowtime.log();
Indiana Jones IV   6.1.2014 10:19:40(1388999980)
Quantum of Solace  6.1.2014 04:46:20(1388979980)
La Dolce Vita   4.1.2014 02:46:20(1388799980)
```

Although the order of the movies collection was mutated, the state of the models re-mained constant. This is important, because movies could be sorted according to dif-ferent criteria, but all movies models are kept in the collection. When filtering a col-lection, this can be different.

Using a single comparator function is somewhat limiting when users want to sort ac-cording to multiple criteria (e.g., showtime, genre, or rating of a movie). Luckily, Un-derscore.js adds sortBy to a Backbone collection. With sortBy, we inject a comparator function, without using a single comparator on a collection.

For sorting movies at Munich Cinema, we need multiple sort functions to sort movies by their rating, showtime, and title. When you invoke sortBy on a collection, you obtain the list of models in a new order.

To use sortBy, write a special function to sort movies by titles. Back in our Movies collection at *app/collection/movies.js*, you can add:

```
Movies = Backbone.Collection.extend({
  // ...

sortByTitle: function() {
  return this.sortBy('title');
}

});
```

After bundling, you can run a sort by invoking sortByTitle:

```
> var Movies = require('movies');
> var movies = new Movies(raw);
> sorted = new Movies(movies.sortByTitle());
> sorted.log();
```

As output, you should get:

```
Argo    3.1.2014 12:39:40 (1388749180)
Avatar   29.12.2013 20:26:20 (1388345180)
Dead Man Down   3.1.2014 19:36:20 (1388774180)
Django Unchained   11.12.2013 17:26:20 (1386779180)
```

In contrast to the first example, the sorted output of one collection is inserted into a new collection. When you have an existing collection, you can simplify sorting to adding new items:

```
> sorted.reset(movies.sortByTitle())
```

The same strategy can be used for sorting movies according to other criteria. To complete the exercise, let's add the following code to *app/collections/movies.js*:

```
sortByRating: function() {
    var sorted = this.sortBy(function(m) {
      return (10 - m.get('rating'));
    });
    return sorted;
},

sortByShowtime: function() {
    return this.sortBy('showtime');
}
```

With sortByRating and sortByShowtime, movies can be sorted according to two more criteria.

To round up the examples, let's wire up these function to the UI. For this, you need to provide some buttons in the UI for sorting. You can define a small view as follows in *app/views/sort.js*:

```
var Backbone = require('backbone');
var SortView = Backbone.View.extend({
```

```
    events: {
      'click #by_title': 'sortByTitle',
      'click #by_rating': 'sortByRating',
      'click #by_showtime': 'sortByShowtime',
    },

    sortByTitle: function(ev) {
      this.movies.reset(this.movies.sortByTitle());
    },

    sortByRating: function(ev) {
      this.movies.reset(this.movies.sortByRating());
    },

    sortByShowtime: function(ev) {
      this.movies.reset(this.movies.sortByShowtime());
    },

    initialize: function() {
      this.movies = this.collection;
    }
  });
  module.exports = SortView;
```

We also need to extend the layout template and make sure the events are properly re-solved. One way to do this is by adding the following to *app/views/layout.js*:

```
render: function() {
  this.$el.html(this.template());
  this.currentDetails.setElement(this.$('#details')).render();
  this.overview.setElement(this.$('#overview')).render();
  this.controls.setElement(this.$('#controls'));
  return this;
},

initialize: function(options) {
  this.overview = new MoviesList({
    collection: options.router.movies,
    router: options.router
  });
  this.controls = new Controls({ collection: options.router.movies });
}
```

And we include a piece of HTML in the layout template:

```
template: _.template('                    \
        <header>                           \
          <a href="#">Home</a>  \
            <nav id="controls"> \
              <button id="by_title">By Title</button>   \
              <button id="by_rating">By Rating</button>\
              <button id="by_showtime">By Showtime</button> \
            </nav>                 \
```

```
        </header>           \
    <div id="overview">     \
    </div>                  \
    <div id="details">      \
    </div>')
```

A user would now be able to sort movies in the DOM according to different criteria. Don't worry that this inline template starts to look awkward. In Chapter 6, you learn how to use a templating engine to keep templates in a separate file. If you haven't followed the examples of this chapter with an editor, you can play with it on the book's website (*http://pipefishbook.com/ch_5/sortui/*).

Filtering

The next goal is to provide filtering options for movies. This will allow users to find movies, for example, that belong to a specific genre. Once the user has selected the appropriate filter options, the movie program should automatically update to show just those movies that meet the chosen criteria.

Let's look briefly at what filtering does. Basically, filtering is an applied set theory, as shown in Figure 5-1. There is a superset containing all elements, and the filtered collections are subsets matching certain criteria. As such, filtering is a transformation or projection from input to output collection.

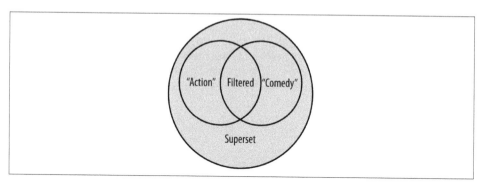

Figure 5-1. Filtering a collection means that collections are transformed; filtered sets only contain items that match certain criteria (e.g., movies from a category "drama," "action," or "comedy")

Based on the view layouts from Chapter 4, we add some filter controls to the controls view. This means that you can add a bit of markup for playing with a filtering action:

```
<div id="filter-controls">
  <select name="genre">
    <option value="all">
        All
    </option>
```

```
    <option value='Drama'>
       Drama
    </option>
    <option value='Action'>
       Action
    </option>
  </select>
</div>
```

When filtering a collection, users dynamically add and remove models. As filtering can destroy the state of a collection, a copy of the original collection must be saved for reference.

The idea of working with a copy (or proxy) of the original set can look as follows. Because a Backbone collection can be initialized by passing models, you can create a copy of the movies collection. This new collection (superset) can be created in the initialization of the layout (i.e., in the initialize(options) function of *app/views/layout.js*):

```
var superset = new Backbone.Collection(options.router.movies.models);
```

This superset can now be used as starting point for filtering models. Imagine how filter controls for genres might get called in *app/views/layouts.js*:

```
this.controls = new Controls({ collection: options.router.movies,
  superset: superset });
```

Next, you can extend the UI for sorting to a general UI for controlling filter and sort. Combining sort and filtering will result in the following view (*./app/views/controls.js*):

```
var Backbone = require('backbone');
var _ = require('underscore');
var $ = Backbone.$;

var ControlsView = Backbone.View.extend({

events: {
   'click #by_title': 'sortByTitle',
   'click #by_rating': 'sortByRating',
   'click #by_showtime': 'sortByShowtime',
   'change select[name="genre"]': 'selectGenre'
},

selectGenre: function(ev) {
   var genre = $("select[name='genre']").val();
   var that = this;
   if (genre === "all") {
     that.collection.reset(that.superset.toJSON());
   }
   else {
     that.collection.reset(that.superset.toJSON());
     this.filterByCategory(genre);
   }
},
```

```
filterByCategory: function(genre) {
  var filtered = this.movies.filter(function(m) {
    return (_.indexOf(m.get('genres'), genre) !== -1)
  });
  this.collection.reset(filtered);
},

sortByTitle: function(ev) {
  this.movies.reset(this.movies.sortByTitle());
},

sortByRating: function(ev) {
  this.movies.reset(this.movies.sortByRating());
},

sortByShowtime: function(ev) {
  this.movies.reset(this.movies.sortByShowtime());
},

  initialize: function(options) {
    this.movies = this.collection;
    this.superset = options.superset;
  }
});
module.exports = ControlsView;
```

Besides the actions for sorting that were discussed in the beginning, a number of new things are included:

- You pass the superset via the options helper and save this for usage later.
- The genres of a movie are stored in a nested array, where you need to filter only on one value. Because this array can potentially contain many values, you use an Underscore.js helper to check the values in the array for a matching genre.
- Before the movies collection is filtered, you reset the collection with the filtered set.

Let's quickly check that we can filter the movie program for any movie. If everything works, all movies without *Action* will be removed from the collection, as we see in Figure 5-2. When we then re-select *All*, we see the original collection. You can also see the example in action on the book's website (*http://pipefishbook.com/ch_5/filterui/*).

From the use of Underscore functions, you see already that building a filter is a bit more advanced than the sorting UI. Apart from mutating the state of the collection, genres can come as a function of the available movies and good filters need to take that into account. Also, we might work with another API endpoint that synchronizes with the Genres collection. These advanced approaches will be a topic for the later chapters.

Figure 5-2. We can now filter and sort movies in the UI; for sorting, we keep all models in a collection, but models are removed for filtering, and we need to save a copy of the original collection

Backbone.Obscura

Sorting and filtering collections are very common, so it is wise to avoid reinventing the wheel. And, by using a plug-in from the Backbone ecosystem, we get an additional strategy to mutate collections for free: pagination.

Backbone.Obscura (*https://github.com/jmorrell/backbone.obscura*) is a plug-in by Jeremy Morell that includes support for sorting, filtering, and paginating. Let's look at how this plug-in can replace a lot of our boilerplate code from before.

To get started with a plug-in, we need to include the plug-in in our Backbone stack. You can add the following dependency with npm:

```
$ npm install backbone.obscura --save
```

The plug-in will replace part of the manual work you did previously and provide helpers to paginate a collection out of the box.

Let's start by requiring Backbone.Obscura in *app/views/layout.js*:

```
Backbone.Obscura = require('backbone.obscura');
```

Once the plug-in is available, it can proxy our movies collection. Backbone.Obscura keeps track of a superset by itself. From the proxy, you can access the original collection by calling `superset()`. Also, Backbone.Obscura delegates events to the proxy as needed.

To initialize the proxy, you wrap the original movies collection as follows in the constructor of *app/views/layout.js*:

```
this.proxy = new Backbone.Obscura(options.router.movies);
```

From here on, you use the proxy in the application for rendering data:

```
this.addView('#overview', new MoviesList({
  collection: this.proxy,
  router: options.router
}));
this.controls = new Controls({ proxy: this.proxy });
```

In *app/views/controls.js*, you can apply the sort functions provided by using `setSort()`:

```
sortByTitle: function(ev) {
  app.movies.setSort("title", "asc");
},

sortByRating: function(ev) {
  app.movies.setSort("rating", "desc");
},

sortByShowtime: function(ev) {
  app.movies.setSort("showtime", "asc");
}
```

And for the filtering, you can use the `filterBy()` method, which can take an attribute or callback function:

```
that.proxy.filterBy(genre, function(movie) {
  var genreFound = _.indexOf(movie.get('genres'), genre.value);
  return (genreFound !== -1);
});
```

With the callback function, advanced filters such as filtering on multiple genres becomes quite easy, too. For example, selecting multiple genres could be done with:

```
selectGenres: function(ev) {
  var that = this;
  that.proxy.resetFilters();
  var genres = _.map($("input[type=checkbox]:checked"), function(genre) {
    that.proxy.filterBy(genre.value, function(m) {
      return (_.findWhere(m.get('genres'), genre.value))
    })
  });
}
```

Last, there is a nice way to remove all filters with:

```
this.proxy.resetFilters();
```

For pagination, you have several helpers, too. To set the number of items on a page, you can use:

```
this.proxy.setPerPage(4);
```

And, to browse the collection, you can do:

```
paginateNext: function() {
  this.proxy.nextPage();
},

paginatePrev: function() {
  this.proxy.prevPage();
}
```

You can play with the demo on the book's website (*http://pipefishbook.com/ch_5/ obscura/*). Figure 5-3 shows how the current interface looks. Note that the filters are now multiple checkboxes, instead of a single select box as they were earlier. Also, we now show the page numbers in the info view. You can find the markup for the checkboxes in the book examples repository at *http://pipefishbook.com*.

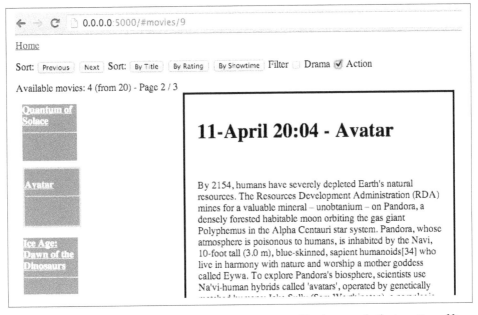

Figure 5-3. With Backbone.Obscura, you can proxy collections such that sorting, filtering, and paginating functions become a piece of cake

Conclusion

In this chapter, you played with important functions to mutate the state of a collection. Both nondestructive (e.g., sorting) and destructive (e.g., filtering) methods were discussed. Then, you met Backbone.Obscura, a plug-in from the Backbone ecosystem that boosts functions of collections for sorting, filtering, and paginating.

So far, our user interface is still a bit basic. In particular, we haven't discussed good ways to use advanced templates for view rendering. Also, as we create more views and collections, automating our workflow for application development becomes important. So, in the next chapter, you will learn important ideas on templating. After having discussed templates, the book will move toward discussing view templates and backend requirements.

CHAPTER 6

Advanced View Templates

So far, you've only used embedded view templates in the code base for Munich Cinema. However, Backbone provides several options to combine advanced HTML templates with Backbone views.

The task of integrating view templates into a Backbone project raises new design questions on an application stack. You could argue that you need support of server-side rendering of views for the first page load or for search engine optimization (SEO) purposes.

For Munich Cinema, support of server-side rendering is not needed. Here, a pure client-side application is sufficient, because our main goal is to provide a subapplication for a better browsing experience. Similar concerns apply if you work on mobile applications or other data-driven interfaces.

In this chapter, we extend the knowledge we've gained in previous chapters regarding how to integrate view templates. Also, we will add some better view templates and a basic build process with Grunt.js. With Grunt.js, we easily can "uglify" frontend assets for better transport.

The following Node-based tools for frontend development will be discussed:

- ECO view templates
- JST view templates
- Grunt, including how to set up a build process

Views and Templates

In the prototype of Munich Cinema, the DOM nodes from Backbone.Views were very basic. By embedding templates in views, the views easily bloat up, as you can observe from the current Layout view. Also, if you collaborate with developers that work on HTML and CSS only, it can often be helpful to have a separate directory for HTML templates only. Last, with a template engine, you can embed a bit of logic, such as loops, to simplify building list elements.

As view templates are often written in an HTML style, you need to compile the raw templates into a syntax that is compatible with JavaScript. The conversion from one syntax to another can often be simplified with so-called build tools, such as Grunt. Workflows and build automation will be discussed again later in the book.

Let's look first at some popular templating engines.

JST

JST stands for JavaScript Templates and is a very popular approach to mix HTML tags with embedded JavaScript.

To include JST templates with Browserify, you need to use a so-called transform plug-in to translate the JST syntax into a JavaScript function. This list (*https://github.com/substack/node-browserify/wiki/list-of-transforms*) provides an overview of supported Browserify transforms.

To transform JST into JavaScript modules, you can use the `jstify` transform (*https://github.com/zertosh/jstify*). First, you must install the plug-in with:

```
$ npm install jstify --save-dev
```

For now, you will need this dependency only for development, hence the `--save-dev`.

Templates are often shared with a web designer colleague, so it is good practice to keep templates in a central place. For this, you will need a new directory to work with the templates:

```
$ mkdir app/templates
```

Next, you can create a JST template to replace the embedded genres filter with the following template *app/templates/genres.html.jst*:

```
<ul class="filter-genres">
  <% _.each(genres, function(name) { %>
    <li>
      <input type="checkbox" name="genres" value="<%= name %>">
        <%= name %>
      </input>
    </li>
  <% }) %>
</ul>
```

You can then `require` the template in a view *app/views/genresFilter.js*, as follows:

```
var Backbone = require('backbone');
var genresTemplate = require('../templates/genres.jst');

// The UI for selecting a Movie Category
var GenresView = Backbone.View.extend({

template: genresTemplate,

render: function() {
  this.$el.html(this.template({genres: this.genres}));
  return this;
},

initialize: function() {
  this.genres = ['Action', 'Drama', 'Comedy'];
}
});
module.exports = GenresView;
```

The genres could again come from outside the view, but right now this is secondary in the discussion.

Now you can use the `browserify` command together with the `jstify` transform:

```
$ browserify ./app/main.js -t jstify > static/bundle.js
```

Note, in other application stacks, there is a global JST object template module. This "JST" object acts as a central object from where all templates can be referenced. For example, this is the default approach in frameworks such as Ruby on Rails and Sprockets, or in Grunt-based build processes, which we will discuss soon:

```
template: JST['genresFilter']
```

To create this JST object, we usually have a build step where the templates are concatenated into a single file and exported as a JST object. Because this step is very similar to preparing an application for deployment, we'll discuss this further in "Grunt" on page 81.

ECO

Another approach to improve building DOM nodes is given by ECO templates. ECO stands for "embedded CoffeeScript." Some prefer the minimal syntax of JavaScript. Also, the template engine can be easily combined with stacks based on Ruby on Rails or Stitch, as ECO is written by the same author, Sam Stephensson. Here's how we install it:

```
$ npm install eco
```

From now on, we can combine the template property in a Backbone.View by requiring an external file. Let's show this on the example of a better GenresFilter.

A view template for the filter might look like:

```
<ul class="filter-genres">
  <% for genre in genres: %>
    <li>
      <input type="checkbox" name="genres" value="<%= name %>">
        <%= name %>
      </input>
    </li>
  <% end %>
</ul>
```

You can compile this template with the `browserify-eco` transform as follows:

```
$ browserify ./app/main.js -t browserify-eco
```

By applying the ECO format, we can write logic such as `for genre in genres`. This will look familiar if you have worked with embedded Ruby or other embedded template approaches before.

Handlebars

With Handlebars templates (*http://handlebarsjs.com/*), you can embed a high amount of logic into a view. We will cover Handlebars in detail again in Chapter 11.

To give you an idea of how Handlebars templates should look, let's rewrite the filter with a Handlebars syntax:

```
<ul class="filter-genres">
{{#each genres}}
  <li>
    <input type="checkbox" name="genres" value="{{ name }}">
      {{ name }}
    </input>
  </li>
{{/each}}
</ul>
```

As you can see, working with templates feels closer to working with HTML than it does to working with JavaScript. Before we apply a better templating in the Munich Cinema example, let's shortly mention other approaches to templating.

React and Others

Backbone can easily be extended with plug-ins or external libraries, which means you can include very advanced strategies for building DOM nodes. A number of strategies are especially interesting:

Backburner (https://github.com/ebryn/backburner.js/)
> When changing multiple DOM nodes at once, it often becomes necessary to control events for rendering in one place. The topic of coalescing properties in views is

currently beyond the scope of the book, but interested readers should investigate Backburner for a possible approach.

React.js (https://github.com/facebook/react)
React.js makes interfaces composable. For this, React.js provides a powerful abstraction, the "Shadow DOM." To start with React.js, you can use your existing Backbone views and simply replace your render function with React.js. As a next step, you could replace HTML templates with React's JSX templates. Browserify supports React views with a "JSX" transform. Further discussion of React.js is currently beyond the scope of this book.

Build Automation

So far, you used the command line and Browserify to bundle JavaScript assets in the web application, but integrating many view templates, tests for code, and CSS styling often require some kind of build processes. Also, you probably will deal with a server process as well as processes for testing your application.

Besides building and serving your application, you probably want to control the quality of your code with JSLint or code beautifiers. And to prepare your application for deployment, you will want to minify the frontend assets for better transport over HTTP.

All these goals are the topics of build automation, and in this section we take a look at Grunt to bundle view templates and support the development of an application.

Having an understanding of build processes is also crucial for so-called isomorphic JavaScript applications, where view templates can be rendered on both the client and server. As an example, the Rendr library (*https://github.com/rendrjs/rendr*) by Spike Brehm provides an application stack based on Backbone, Grunt, and Browserify, where Backbone views can be rendered on both the client and server.

 As Gruntfiles (the description of a build process) can look a bit complicated at first, some developers prefer to stay with simpler Makefiles or Gulp. While the role of Makefiles in JavaScript projects is nicely discussed by James Coglan (*http://bit.ly/1AbRlcL*), you can find a short overview on Gulp here (*http://thinkingonthinking.com/intro-to-gulp/*).

Grunt

Grunt (*https://github.com/gruntjs/grunt*) is a widely popular task runner from the Node ecosystem. By using a Gruntfile, you can automate build tasks and include tasks for managing different tasks, such as running a server process, bundling templates, and testing JavaScript. The syntax for Grunt tasks can be a bit confusing at first. For details you should consult one of the many tutorials on the topic.

Working with Grunt has become very popular in the world of frontend development, and a number of resources exist to help you see the many ways that Grunt can support you. We will also return to the discussion of Grunt in Chapter 10, in which we'll look at its role in bundling applications based on RequireJS.

Grunt is controlled from the command line. The tasks in a Gruntfile can be defined for different modes for operations, such as development, testing, or production. The concepts behind Grunt are closely related to a Makefile or its derivatives Rakefile or Ant, in Ruby or Java.

You can use Grunt's built-in tasks that are optimized for frontend JavaScript development, or you can extend Grunt with plug-ins. Build tasks can be as easy as syntax checking of source files to more complicated operations as preprocessing styles, or preparing files for production. All the tasks are defined in a so-called *Gruntfile*.

You can install Grunt with:

```
$ npm install -g grunt
```

For now, we want to have Grunt support for the following tasks in development mode:

- Run a server process, and watch the server file for changes.
- Concatenate and bundle Handlebars view templates, and watch these files for changes.

To achieve these goals, you also need tasks that come from Grunt plug-ins. To quickly set up your dependencies, you can add the following new dependencies in *package.json*:

```
"dependencies": {
  ...
  "grunt-browserify": "~2.0.7",
  "grunt-contrib-watch": "~0.6.1",
  "grunt-contrib-handlebars": "~0.7.0",
  "nodemon": "~1.0.17",
  "handlebars": "~1.3.0"
}
```

These dependencies are installed in our project folder with:

```
$ npm install
```

As you can see, you also fetch the dependencies nodemon and handlebars. With node mon, the server process is automatically reloaded when a file changes. The Handlebars dependency supports you in translating hbs view templates to JavaScript.

Next, let's look at the Gruntfile. A Gruntfile can become quite large, and sometimes it can be understood if you work your way up, from bottom to top.

First, there are the tasks of a Gruntfile that can be called as commands from the command line. For development purposes, we are mainly interested in a server task, where all changes are observed and translated into new outputs as appropriate. This translates to the following snippet in the *Gruntfile.js* of your project directory:

```
grunt.registerTask('compile', ['handlebars', 'browserify']);

// Run the server and watch for file changes
grunt.registerTask('server', ['compile', 'runNode', 'watch']);

// Default task
grunt.registerTask('default', ['compile']);
```

These tasks can be defined recursively. For example, the runNode task can look like:

```
grunt.registerTask('runNode', function () {
  grunt.util.spawn({
    cmd: 'node',
    args: ['./node_modules/.bin/nodemon', 'server.js'],
    opts: {
      stdio: 'inherit'
    }
  }, function () {
    grunt.fail.fatal(new Error("nodemon quit"));
  });
});
```

while the other tasks can be included from a plug-in:

```
grunt.loadNpmTasks('grunt-browserify');
grunt.loadNpmTasks('grunt-contrib-handlebars');
grunt.loadNpmTasks('grunt-contrib-watch');

grunt.registerTask('runNode', function () {
  grunt.util.spawn({
    cmd: 'node',
    args: ['./node_modules/.bin/nodemon', 'server.js'],
    opts: {
      stdio: 'inherit'
    }
  }, function () {
    grunt.fail.fatal(new Error("nodemon quit"));
  });
});
```

Last, tasks can be configured. This configuration takes up the most space in a Gruntfile. Let's first look at the configuration of the Browserify task:

```
browserify: {
  options: {
    debug: true,
    aliasMappings: [
      {
        cwd: 'app/',
```

```
        src: ['**/*.js'],
        dest: 'app/'
      }
    ]
  },
  app: {
    src: [ 'app/**/*.js' ],
    dest: 'static/bundle.js'
  }
}
```

And, to configure the tasks for watch and Handlebars templates, you can add:

```
watch: {
  scripts: {
    files: 'app/**/*.js',
    tasks: ['browserify'],
    options: {
      interrupt: true
    }
  },
  templates: {
    files: 'app/**/*.hbs',
    tasks: ['handlebars'],
    options: {
      interrupt: true
    }
  },
},
handlebars: {
  compile: {
    options: {
      namespace: false,
      commonjs: true,
      processName: function(filename) {
        return filename.replace('app/templates/', '').replace('.hbs', '');
      }
    },
    src: "app/templates/**/*.hbs",
    dest: "app/templates/compiledTemplates.js"
  }
}
```

Last, you must wrap all the code in an initConfig function, and the resulting *Grunt-file.js* should look like this example file (*https://github.com/pipefishbook/ch_6/blob/master/grunt/Gruntfile.js*).

Other popular tasks include jshint, which performs a syntax check:

```
jshint: {
  options: {
    curly: true
  },
```

```
  gruntfile: {
    src: 'Gruntfile.js'
  }
}
```

and a task for cleaning up previous builds:

```
// Clean public folder
clean: {
  all: ["dist/*.js"]
}
```

We can check that the Gruntfile is set up correctly with:

```
$ jslint Gruntfile.js
$ grunt --help
```

Running grunt help returns a list of tasks that come from the *gruntfile.js*:

```
Available tasks
    browserify  Grunt task for browserify. *
    handlebars  Compile handlebars templates and partials. *
         watch  Run predefined tasks whenever watched files change.
       runNode  Custom task.
       compile  Alias for "handlebars", "browserify" tasks.
        server  Alias for "compile", "runNode", "watch" tasks.
       default  Alias for "compile" task.
```

The default task is run if we call grunt without arguments.

 Depending on the strategies for packaging assets, a Gruntfile can become rather large. It often makes sense to modularize your Gruntfile by having configurations in external files. A number of developers share their preferred application structure with a Gruntfile, too. For an example of a basic Gruntfile for a Backbone app, go to *https:// github.com/kud/marrow*. We will see more ways for automation in Chapter 10.

Running our grunt server task results in:

```
$ grunt server
Running "handlebars:compile" (handlebars) task
File app/templates/compiledTemplates.js created.

Running "browserify:app" (browserify) task

Running "runNode" task

Running "watch" task
Waiting...
15 Apr 19:25:21 - [nodemon] v1.0.17
15 Apr 19:25:21 - [nodemon] to restart at any time, enter `rs`
```

```
15 Apr 19:25:21 - [nodemon] watching: *.*
15 Apr 19:25:21 - [nodemon] starting `node server.js`

Pushstate server started on port 5000
```

Now, when you change the files in the application, the application is automatically browserified, and you can have faster feedback on your development. Let's add a reference to Handlebars as follows:

```
var Handlebars = require('handlebars');
var Templates = require('templates/compiledTemplates')(Handlebars);
```

and a template for movies in *app/templates/movies.hbs*:

```
<h1>
  <a href="/movies/{{ id }}">
    {{ title }}
  </a>
</h1>
<hr>
```

If you observe the terminal output, you should see that the template is automatically precompiled for you, too.

Conclusion

In this chapter, you learned about advanced approaches to DOM manipulation with JST and ECO templates. You also learned to browserify templates with a transform. You then met build automation wiht Grunt.js and a very basic Gruntfile.js to support you with application development.

Now that we've applied better templating to it, our web application is almost ready for deployment. You still need to learn more about APIs, and how to connect those to your Backbone models and collections to build a fully working web application. As build processes are an important part of JavaScript web applications, you will also learn more about workflow automation in Chapter 10. In addition, you will be introduced to more Backbone plug-ins for special types of interactions in the following chapters.

CHAPTER 7

Synchronizing State

The previous chapters offered a preliminary glance of state in the browser. We covered the basics of Backbone views, models, and collections to manage state. But to build a real app, you must connect your collections and models to an API. These are the enhancements of Backbone collections that we haven't yet discussed.

One of the main purposes of a Backbone collection is to fetch new information (or state) over a network. To understand the basic ideas here, you need to understand a bit of RESTful principles for APIs and how Backbone maps these internally to the API of collections and models.

In the case of the Munich Cinema example, when a collection manages tens or hundreds of movies, new questions on filtering and sorting them arise. Dealing with more data also takes an important role in our customer's project: Munich Cinema wants to allow its customers to search for movies by release date and genres. To help customers decide which movies to watch, Munich Cinema prepared ratings of movies that might further distill a movie search.

So we must expand our application with a number of features. In this chapter, we'll cover the following:

- Setting up a mock of a RESTful API
- Enabling fetching of remote data from an API
- Dealing with time effects around fetching
- Understanding the basics of hosted API services

Fetching Remote Movies

So far, the examples were based on a few movies directly linked with the initial page load. Munich Cinema's movie program is much larger though, especially during festival season. For this, users can select movie genres or browse lists with with many more movies. Let's look at important ideas behind requests for more movies with Backbone.

RESTful Web Services

Web services make data over a network accessible—for example, to query information. In most application stacks based on Backbone.js, the user interface is the client of a web service. The part of Backbone.js that handles access to RESTful web services is Backbone.Sync. By default, Backbone.js expects a web service to follow the RESTful principles. Let's have a look at Figure 7-1 to see what it means.

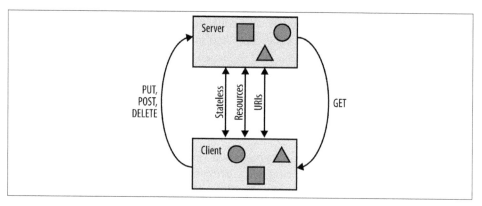

Figure 7-1. In a RESTful web service, we use the basic verbs GET, POST, PUT, and DELETE from HTTP to transfer state between client and server—addressability, representations, and statelessness are some core ideas for RESTful API design; in HTML, links and forms are the main tools to modify state, but with Backbone.js, you can reference state with collections and models

Let's quickly review some of the core concepts of a RESTful web service:

Statelessness

> Transferring and changing state over a network is the origin of the REpresentational State Transfer concept, or REST. Yet, resources should be stateless with respect to requests from clients, meaning the application state in a browser does not affect the response of the server. Modifying state of a resource, however, is possible with POST, PUT, or DELETE requests. Modifying client state from the server is done with GET requests.

Different representations
> A client accesses a *representation* of a resource, not the resource itself. In general, a server exposes different representations. For a Backbone.js client, we are mainly interested in a JSON representation, but the same data might be requested in HTML or XML. While HTML representations are convenient for humans, JSON and XML are representations that can be more easily used by machines such as Backbone.js-based clients, or an RSS reader.

Addressability
> In a network of information, information resources should clearly be identified with a URI, a uniform resource identifier. For example, to show data about movies, we would define a clear path for how to get these in the application, similar to a filename in a filesystem. A URI is basically the name of a resource and acts as input to clients of web services.

With these principles, we build web architectures that focus on connecting resources. As such, we can easily build different (Backbone.js) clients acting on the same resources on a server.

For example, for Munich Cinema, we developed a client to browse movies. Similarly, we could develop an admin interface that allows us to modify movies or another interface for sharing feedback of movies on a dashboard.

Mocking an API

Instead of using remote data from a remote data store, it can make sense to mock responses for data first. By mocking API data, frontend and backend development can be separated—and you can continue developing the Backbone application without thinking too much about server-side requirements. For the purposes of the book, a mock API can help to illustrate timing effects when loading data.

There are two approaches we can take: mocking an API on the server or mocking an API in the browser. You already have some experience with using npm, so we'll discuss mocking an API on the server first.

To mock data from a remote data store, we use the canned library (*https://github.com/ sideshowcoder/canned*) written by Philip Fehre. The idea of this library is to map files from a directory to HTTP requests.

For example, by having files in the *./api/movies/* directory, you would automatically get responses as follows:

```
File                             | HTTP Path
---------------------------------+-----------------
./movies/index.get.json          | GET /api/movies
./movies/any.get.json            | GET /api/movies/:id
```

You can install canned with:

```
$ npm install canned --save-dev
```

Next, you can create some example movies in the *api/movies/index.get.json* file. One example looks like:

```
{
  "title": "Ice Age: Dawn of the Dinosaurs",
  "director": "Carlos Saldanha",
  "rating": 0,
  "showtime": 1388279380,
  "description": "Ellie and Manny are expecting their
   first child, and Manny is nervously obsessed with
   making life perfect and safe for Ellie. ... ",
  "id": 10,
  "year": 2009,
  "length": 94,
  "genres": [
   "Animation",
   "Action",
   "Adventure"
  ]
}
```

Canned can be called stand-alone or combined with middleware applications in a server stack. This will allow us to serve static files too, besides the API data. Therefore, our server in a *./server.js* file can look as follows:

```
var http = require('http');

// Setup the can to mock data
var canned = require('canned');
var opts = { cors: true, logger: process.stdout };
can = canned('.', opts);  // canned configuration

var express = require('express');
var app = express();

// adding middlewares
app.use(express.static(__dirname + '/static'));
app.use(can);

// startup server
http.createServer(app).listen(5000);
```

You can start this server with:

```
$ node server.js
```

When you now make a request to the */api/movies* path, you are ready to serve movies data with canned.

To check that your setup is working, you have several options. First, you could use curl, a command-line HTTP client:

```
$ curl 0.0.0.0:5000/api/movies
```

Alternatively, you could open the URL *http://0.0.0.0:5000/api/movies* in your web browser.

And in the context of a Backbone app, you could set up an Ajax request with jQuery in *app/main.js*:

```
$.ajax({
    url: "/api/movies",
    headers: {"content-type": "application/json"}
});
```

A working API setup should return a result similar to Figure 7-2.

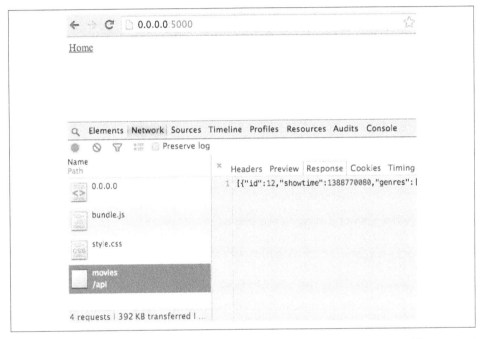

Figure 7-2. To see the API mock for a server in action, you can run an Ajax request with jQuery and inspect the Network tab in the browser console

Once this setup is working, let's delve deeper into the enhancements of a Backbone collection to fetch data from an API.

Basic Sync and Fetch

Backbone collections and models provide important enhancements to work with a RESTful API through Backbone.Sync. Conceptually, you can see the place for Backbone.Sync in Figure 7-3.

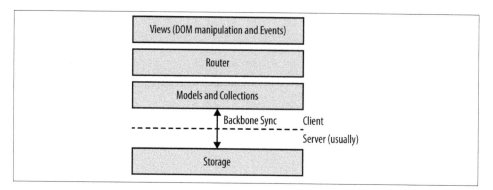

Figure 7-3. In the previous chapters, we discussed mainly DOM manipulation and tracking basic state with Backbone models and collections; to synchronize state over the network, we need to talk about Backbone.Sync

Every request from and to servers pass through Backbone.Sync. State in collections can not only be synchronized through a RESTful JSON API but also via sockets, XML, or with an HTML5 `localStorage` adapter.

However, for the Munich Cinema example, the main use case is synchronizing state through HTTP. To synchronize state via an API, you need to solve a number of problems:

- A Backbone.Model resolves data on the server by using a primary key. Backbone.Sync adds an ID to requests when data is stored.
- The attributes of Backbone models will be serialized as JSON. Backbone.Syncs provides help to serialize and de-serialize data.
- Last, we must set some HTTP headers, such as `content-type`, so that the interpretation at the other end of the line understands what is going on. The HTTP headers are also managed by Backbone.Sync.

Backbone.Sync manages actions for writing and reading data from a server. For this, Backbone defines its own verbs: `create`, `read`, `update`, and `delete` with the following mappings to the routes of a RESTful API:

```
Backbone verb  vs  RESTful API endpoint
create movie <--> POST /movies
read movie   <--> GET /movies[/id]
```

```
update movie <--> PUT /movies/id
delete movie <--> DELETE /movies/id
```

By default, Backbone.Sync expects the JSON going and coming from a server to comply with the following pattern:

```
[{ 'id': 1, 'title: 'The Artist', ... }, ... ]
```

This means that you don't have root elements indicating the name of the movies collection, for example. Some APIs, however, use a JSON syntax with a root element. For example, many web applications that are based on older versions of Ruby on Rails would deliver JSON in the following syntax:

```
{ "movies": [ { "movie" : { "id" : 1, ... } } ] }
```

For such kinds of APIs, you must take care of parsing the raw data that comes out from Backbone.Sync. Parsing raw data also applies to situations where you are working with non-RESTful APIs, such as data from sockets. For those cases, you can overwrite parts (or the complete) synching behavior.

> The documentation will be a good start if you need to overwrite the default Backbone sync behavior (e.g., when you want to connect application state to websockets). The annotated source code of Backbone.js (*http://backbonejs.org/docs/backbone.html#section-130*) has a nice list of use cases when overwriting Backbone.Sync, which might be important.

To start working with an API, we first explore the mapping of Backbone.Sync to "read" movies. The data is provided by `canned` with the setup described in "Mocking an API" on page 89.

First, the `Movies` collection can be extended such that data is read from the API instead of embedded JSON. To do this, you add a `url` property to the collection. This `url` property points a collection to an API endpoint as follows in *app/collection/movies.js*:

```
var Movies = Backbone.Collection.extend({
  model: require('models/movie'),

  url: '/api/movies',

  // ... same as before
});
module.exports = Movies;
```

Let's bundle the collection up with the following `browserify` command:

```
$ browserify -r ./app/collections/movies:movies > static/movies.js
```

and add the file to *static/index.html*:

```
<script src="movies"></script>
```

Now you are ready to experiment in the browser console:

```
> Movies = require('collections/movies');
> movies = new Movies();
```

To read remote data and populate a collection, Backbone provides the fetch() command. By invoking fetch(), an Ajax request is made to the url path as defined in */api/ movies*. The response is provided by canned, and you can quickly observe new data in the Backbone collection:

```
> movies.fetch()
```

As a response you should see:

```
XHR finished loading: GET "http://0.0.0.0:5000/api/movies"
```

and the collection should be populated:

```
> movies.size()
20
```

However, what looks simple can quickly become more complicated. First, there are a number of events that can result from fetch(). Let's first learn about these.

If you activate again the events monitor from "Basic Events" on page 34, you will see that fetch triggers the following events:

```
request
add // for each new model
sort
sync
```

Often, you want to hook into the add event to render new information from an API. In case of populating a model, you will see a change event. It can be necessary to observe the events request and sync, too—for example, to notify observers that new data is available or that loading of data has stopped.

To illustrate the effects of request and sync events, you could hook into these events to see how long it takes to fetch data:

```
beginSync: function() {
  console.log("before sync: " + Date.now());
},

finishSync: function() {
  console.log("after sync: " + Date.now());
},

initialize: function() {
  this.on('request', this.beginSync);
  this.on('sync', this.finishSync);
}
```

If you fetch new data now, you can see from the browser console that it takes just some fractions of milliseconds to complete loading movies on the development machine.

Alternatively, you could hook into `request` and `sync` and show a small spinner while movies are loaded. For showing a spinner, you would add a new HTML element with class `.movies-loading` that contains a spinning wheel or loading animation.

Then, you could hook into the collection loading events from *app/views/layout.js*. When the loading starts (a `request` event is triggered), the loading div with class `.movies-loading` is shown. And, when the loading stops (a `sync` event is triggered), the loading div is faded out. This idea translates to the following code outline:

```
// start spinner
beginSync: function(){
    $('.movies-loading').fadeIn({duration: 100});
},
// stop spinner
finishSync: function(){
    $('.movies-loading').fadeOut({duration: 100});
}
```

The behavior and events of `fetch` can be influenced by some options. First, you can add `{reset: true}` to clear a collection before it is populated. If you try this:

```
> movies.fetch({reset: true})
```

You can observe the events: `request`, `reset`, and `sync`.

Also, `fetch()` accepts a number of options from the collection `set` command: these are `add`, `remove`, and `merge`, and work as follows.

For example, with `{merge: false}` you can avoid overwriting existing models. To see this, you can prepopulate a `Movies` collection with a dummy model as follows in the browser:

```
> movies.add({id: 12, title: "my test"})
```

Now, when you fetch the collection with:

```
> movies.fetch({merge: false})
```

you can see that collection will be populated with 20 models, but only 19 add events will be fired.

Also, `fetch()` accepts parameters that can directly be passed to an Ajax call. For example, in *app/collections/movies.js*, you can define a function `fetchPage()` to fetch a certain page in a collection:

```
fetchPage: function(num) {
    return this.fetch({data: {page: num}});
}
```

If you try this function in the browser, you can see:

```
> movies.fetchPage(2)
XHR finished loading: GET "http://0.0.0.0:5000/api/movies?page=2".
```

This behavior can be useful if you want to provide server-side support for pagination of collections.

Modifying the way an Ajax request is made also works for HTTP headers. Using HTTP headers is especially interesting for passing meta information of an app to a server.

To illustrate some points about asynchronous effects of loading data, let's imagine a custom HTTP header to simulate a delay. A delay parameter could be passed with a HTTP header, which can then be processed at the server. To define a `fetch()` function with a delay, you could pass a header `X-DELAY` as follows:

```
delayedFetch: function(delay) {
    return this.fetch({headers: {"X-DELAY": delay}});
}
```

The `X-DELAY` header can then be read out at the server and cause an artifical delay in the response. To see this idea in action, you can add the following middleware application to *server.js*:

```
app.use(function(req, res, next) {
  var delay = parseFloat(req.headers['x-delay']);
  if (delay) {
    setTimeout(function() {
      next();
    }, delay);
  } else {
    next();
  }
});
```

Now, if you restart the server and go back to the browser, you can run:

```
> movies.delayedFetch(2000)
```

And, you should see that it now takes two seconds to populate a collection. With these background concepts, let's look closer at problems caused by the asynchronous operation of JavaScript.

Asynchronous Effects

It takes time to transport data over a network, so working with remote data brings in a hidden time dependency into our application. Dealing with time dependencies might be new if you are accustomed to the "blocking" behavior of programming statements that are common in programming languages such as Java or Ruby.

With the "nonblocking" behavior of JavaScript, applications quickly run into asynchronous effects between data transport and code execution. You must take into account that transport of data over a network, which takes a couple of milliseconds, is different than the time for executing JavaScript statements in a browser, which takes only a fraction of milliseconds.

To illustrate the effects of high-latency, low-bandwith network connections, let's experiment a bit with a small simulator.

In the previous section, we wrote a function delayedFetch(). To examine the effects of time on the collection state, we process the size of the collection at different times with the following probe in *app/probe.js*:

```
simTransport = function(movies, simDelay, probeDelay) {
  movies.reset();
  movies.delayedFetch(simDelay);
  window.setTimeout(function() {
    console.log('Probe delay: ' + probeDelay + ' milliseconds.');
    console.log('Simulation delay: ' + simDelay + ' milliseconds.');
    console.log('Collection size: ' + movies.size());
  }, probeDelay);
}
module.exports = simTransport;
```

You can bundle this probe up with:

```
$ browserify -r ./app/probe.js:probe > static/probe.js
```

We first check what happens if we probe the data before it arrives, at around one second after the fetch:

```
> simTransport(movies, 2000, 1000)
Probe delay: 1000 milliseconds.
Simulation delay: 2000 milliseconds.
Collection size: 0
```

Appropriately, the size of the collection is still 0, although we might have expected a populated collection. Simply put, the response time for the remote data takes a couple of milliseconds, while we check the collection size too early.

Without further precautions, we will get errors in the UI. One option to get the correct population is to wait longer. Let's see what happens at three seconds after the fetch:

```
> simTransport(movies, 2000, 3000)
Probe delay: 3000 milliseconds.
Simulation delay: 2000 milliseconds.
Collection size: 20
```

Indeed, we get the expected size for the collection. But guessing network latency is not really an approach to base our engineering efforts upon. We need to find better mechanisms that will allow the loading event to finish.

A first approach to avoid asynchronous problems is to pass a callback function to `fetch`. This can look like:

```
movies.reset();
movies.fetch({ success: function(results) {
    console.log("Collection size: " + movies.size());
  }
});
```

The `success` callback is automatically called when the Ajax call has been succesfully finished.

Callbacks can be hard to read, especially when exceptions occur within a callback, so there is another approach we can use. This alternative approach is the "deferred" syntax that is supported by jQuery.

The basic idea is that instead of letting fetch return an uncertain result, we return a representation of the asynchronous operation, a promise. We can chain this promise with callbacks that should be executed when an operation finishes.

To see this callback idea in action, let's instantiate an empty `movies` collection in the browser and do the following:

```
> var deferred = movies.fetch();
> deferred.done(function() { console.log(movies.size()) });
```

We first bind the fetch to a deferred variable and ensure then that data is loaded with the `done()` method. The size of the collection is now correct without using error-prone guesswork. We can also respond to problems while fetching a movie with the `fail()` method.

Note that calling `done()` multiple times on a promise always yields the same resolved value (i.e., another "sync" operation will not be run after the promise was resolved). This may prevent multiple Ajax requests and may have advantages, depending on the application you are working on.

The full example can be found on the book's GitHub page (*https://github.com/pipefish book/ch_7/tree/master/fetch*).

 We will return to promises when we build our data backend in a later chapter. You can also see *Learning jQuery Deferreds* (O'Reilly, 2013) by Terry Jones and Nicholas H. Tollervey.

Firebase

To round out the basics of fetching remote data, let's point the `Movies` collection to a hosted service.

There are a number of "noBackend" providers offering API hosting that can take away the pains to build and maintain a backend yourself. In this case, you can apply some ideas of this chapter and fetch data from a hosted backend service.

Let's look at an approach to drive your Backbone application with Firebase, one of the popular backend-as-a-service providers. In the next chapter, we get more into API details, when your application requires its own backend design.

To get started with Firebase, you can signup with your GitHub account or simply with your email. On Firebase's dashboard, you then can create as many apps as you like, and there is a free plan available for developing projects.

To have collections and models talk with Firebase, you need to include the Firebase *sync* adapter, which is provided by the Backfire module.

You can get Backfire with the following `npm` command:

```
$ npm install client-firebase --save-dev
```

Now, you can include the sync adapter for Firebase in the `Movies` collection:

```
var Backbone = require('backbone');
Backbone.Firebase = require('./backbone_firebase');
```

To reference movies from Firebase, you can make the `Movies` collection reference Firebase as follows:

```
var Movies = Backbone.Firebase.Collection.extend({
  model: Movie,
  firebase: "https://movies-demo.firebaseio.com/movies",
  // ... same as previously
});
```

From here on, the Firebase `sync()` function takes over. With some minor adaptations, you can get the example of Munich Cinema running, and you can see a demo on the book's website (*http://pipefishbook.com/ch_7/firebase/#*).

With Firebase, you now have a dashboard to easily import more movies and track movies usage. You can also wire up Firebase with other APIs via Zapier to trigger sending emails or other tasks. This might be interesting for some applications, but for others, you want to build your API yourself. This will be the topic of the next chapter.

Conclusion

In this chapter, you made quite some progress toward a full, single-page application that fetches data from a remote data store.

To prevent developing a full backend at this stage, we saw a strategy to mock a RESTful API with `canned`. We then used the mock API to learn about different approaches to populate the `Movies` collection over a network. First, we learned about the basic events that are evolved. Then, we discussed the different options to influence `fetch()` for different needs. We covered asynchronous effects and how to use a promise to prevent making multiple Ajax requests.

We also saw an approach for building web apps with Backbone.js with Firebase. Firebase is a backend-as-a-service provider and allows you to easily access and manage data over an API. Backend-as-a-service does not work for every application. That is why the next chapter brings in more ideas to build APIs yourself and will also discuss some strategies for authentication of an application with Backbone.js.

CHAPTER 8

Basic API Concerns

In the last chapter, you used an API that was "canned" to learn about populating a collection with `fetch()`. Since Backbone.js is backend agnostic, you could work with any programming language or data store to build a "real" application stack. However, with the advances of Node and JavaScript, some of the concepts that apply to Backbone at the client equally apply when building APIs or connecting to data stores at the server.

Even if your use case does not require an isomorphic application design, where logic for templating and data validation can be shared, the concepts of this chapter should help you understand more enhancements of Backbone models and collections to "write" state to a remote server.

To persist state with Backbone, we delve deeper into concepts from API development. This is why this chapter on general persistence, and the next chapter on authentication, move the development of Munich Cinema more and more toward full stack JavaScript application development.

Our discussion on fetching movies is extended to storing votes on movies. In general, changing application state also requires discussion on authenticating users. But to simplify the discussion in this chapter, we let users vote on movies without authentication. Then, in the next chapter, authentication will be discussed.

To store state from the client at a server, we first replace the mock API with a Movies API based on Restify and JavaScript promises based on Bluebird. We then connect the Backbone application to the extended API and discuss further enhancements of Backbone models and collections.

Therefore, this chapter explores the following topics:

- Building a RESTful API with Restify for voting on movies
- Using a Proxy middleware to connect a separate API process
- Data sources

Backend Services

While the user interface of a web application is a service that heavily depends on static files (JavaScript and CSS), the design of a backend service (API) is heavily shaped by the type of data stores. In the classical "LAMP" (Linux-Apache-MySQL-PHP) applications stacks, relational database such as MySQL or Postgres influence how data is stored and queried.

Also, in the Munich Cinema application stack, it would be possible to build a Movies service around a relational database based on an object-relational-mapper (ORM). You could either use a different programming language, or proceed (as we will do later) with JavaScript.

 If you want to use JavaScript with a relational database, you might want to look at the Bookshelf ORM (*http://bookshelfjs.org/*). Written by Tim Griesser, the project borrows a number of abstractions, such as models and collections, from the Backbone data layer.

However, discussing the concepts and ideas of backend services would quickly explode the scope of this book. What we can discuss are a number of concepts that influence the setup of Backbone models and collections. Also, it is important to discuss ideas around separating frontend and API service. Even if you will work with an isomorphic JavaScript app, concepts for connecting a data store will be important.

For operations on data stores with JavaScript, such as querying or writing, we face the same time dependency problems as we discussed in "Asynchronous Effects" on page 96.

Hopefully, the ideas in this chapter can help you understand current projects and discussions to try out some nonrelational data stores too, such as Redis, ArangoDB, or MongoDB.

Proxies

When you are developing an API, you often will require working with multiple processes—for example, for running services for the user interface, the API, and a data store.

In this chapter, we will mainly work with two processes. The frontend process takes all incoming HTTP requests, but requests starting with */api* will be proxied to the API process.

 Working with client and API in isolation is also possible with CORS or "cross origin resource sharing" policies. Unfortunately, older web browsers do not support that W3C recommendation (*http://www.w3.org/TR/cors/*). Piotr Sarnacki's blog post "Client and API Isolation" (*http://bit.ly/1nlsvUe*) includes a good discussion on working with a CORS setup.

To proxy requests from one process to another with Node, you can install the proxy middleware with:

```
$ npm install proxy-middleware --save
```

You can add the proxy middleware in *./server.js* as follows:

```
var http = require('http');
var express = require('express');
var app = express();
var logger = require('morgan');  // to log requests
var url = require('url');
var proxy = require('proxy-middleware');

app.use(logger({ immediate: true, format: 'dev' }));

// The proxy is added with this line:
app.use('/api', proxy(url.parse('http://0.0.0.0:5001/api/')));

app.use(express.static(__dirname + '/static'));

var port = 5000;
http.createServer(app).listen(port, function() {
  console.log('Frontend listening at %s', port);
});
```

With the line:

```
app.use('/api', proxy(url.parse('http://0.0.0.0:5001/api/')));
```

you proxy requests from the server process `0.0.0.0:5000/api` to the API process running at `0.0.0.0:5001/api`. How this API process looks, and how Backbone collections and models can store state, will be clear in a second.

 For some setups, you might want to proxy a RESTful interface of a database directly. For example, the ArangoDB multipurpose data store provides an easy way to mount RESTful APIs with a package called Foxx (*https://www.arangodb.org/foxx*).

To make starting your development environment easy, you could extend your Gruntfile to manage the frontend and backend services. As explained in "Grunt" on page 81, you can register tasks to run the two processes automatically as follows:

```
grunt.registerTask('runFrontend', function () {
  grunt.util.spawn({
    cmd: 'node',
    args: ['./node_modules/.bin/nodemon', 'server.js'],
    opts: {
      stdio: 'inherit'
    }
  }, function () {
    grunt.fail.fatal(new Error("nodemon quit"));
  });
});
grunt.registerTask('runAPI', function () {
  grunt.util.spawn({
    cmd: 'node',
    args: ['./node_modules/.bin/nodemon', 'api.js'],
    opts: {
      stdio: 'inherit'
    }
  }, function () {
    grunt.fail.fatal(new Error("nodemon quit"));
  });
});

// Include both processes in the server task:
grunt.registerTask('server', ['compile', 'runFrontend', 'runAPI', 'watch']);
```

Before running `grunt server`, let's build the Movie services in ./api.js.

Building a Movies Service

When building an API with Node.js, the Restify library (*https://github.com/mcavage/node-restify*) by Mark Cavage is a good choice. Restify is very similar to Express.js but keeps it simpler when it comes to building RESTful APIs.

To continue with the API example from Chapter 7, we replace the setup of canned with a small API variation based on Restify.

To set up the Restify server, you can type the following command:

```
$ npm install restify --save
```

The specification on our first API endpoints would be:

```
GET /api/genres
Return all movie genres

GET /api/movies
Return all movies
```

As a first step, we can serve both resources from the *movies.json* file and set up a basic Restify server in *./api.js*:

```javascript
// Our main API server is powered by restify
var restify = require('restify');
var _ = require('underscore');

var movies = require('./movies.json');

// Similar to Express.js, we create a server with Restify
var server = restify.createServer({ name: 'movies' })

// Adding middleware to process HTTP bodies
server
  .use(restify.fullResponse())
  .use(restify.bodyParser())

// The main API route for movies
server.get('/api/movies', function (req, res, next) {
  res.send(movies);
})

// The API route to extract a genres of movies
server.get('/api/genres', function (req, res, next) {
  var genres = _.chain(movies)
                .map(function(movie) {
                    return movie.genres
                })
                .flatten()
                .uniq()
                .value();
    res.send(genres);
})

var port = process.env.PORT || 5000;
server.listen(port, function () {
  console.log('%s listening at %s', server.name, server.url)
})
```

We can run this server with:

```
$ node api.js
```

Note that we are not simply sending JSON for the genres. Rather, we derive the data with some methods from Underscore.js. That this setup works can be checked with a curl request to genres:

```
$ curl 0.0.0.0:5000/api/genres
["Drama","Comedy","Action","Adventure","Fantasy","Family","Crime","Animation",
 "Mystery","Thriller","Sci-Fi","Western","Biography","History"]
```

Wrapping a Data Store

Our next goal is to bring the idea of "data store" into the API. The main purpose of a data stores is to improve querying and indexing of data.

For example, if our server managed hundreds or thousands of movies, we would add some parameters for pagination (e.g., by adding skip and limit parameters to address a certain page of movies). The processing of these parameters in the backend goes beyond the scope of this book, but in "Basic Sync and Fetch" on page 92, you saw how query parameters could be passed to an API.

What you will learn, however, in this section are basic concepts of dynamic HTTP responses with JavaScript. Let's adapt the route for /api/movies:

```javascript
var restify = require('restify');

var server = restify.createServer({ name: 'movies' });

// We'll play with a simple in-memory data store
var DS = require('./DS.js');
var ds = new DS();

server
  .use(restify.fullResponse())
  .use(restify.bodyParser())

// This is our first API endpoint
server.get('/api/movies', function (req, res, next) {
    // We return all movies from the database
    // ... and we'll see how in a second with:

    // return ds.allMovies()
    //     .then(function(m) { res.send(m); })
    //     .catch(function(err) { res.send(500, err) });
});

// This is our second API endpoint
server.get("/api/movies/:key", function(req, res, next) {
    res.send(400, "pending");
})

var port = process.env.PORT || 5000;
server.listen(port, function () {
    console.log('%s listening at %s', server.name, server.url)
})
```

Right now, the important lines are the ones that set up a database service:

```javascript
var DS = require('./DS.js');
var ds = new DS();
```

How the data store DS.js looks will be the main topic of this chapter.

When working with the nonblocking environment of JavaScript on the server, we face similar problems as we discussed in "Asynchronous Effects" on page 96 on the client. As previously, we will introduce JavaScript promises to deal with pending (unresolved) states from asynchronous operations.

Although promises will be natively supported with the upcoming JavaScript ECMA6 specification, it should be noted that some developers prefer working with callbacks only. Callbacks and promises should *not* be combined.

Promises are constructs to reason about code outcomes in the future. Without knowing how long code execution will take, you can ensure that statements run in a certain order. Or, when statements fail, you can easily recover an operation. This is similar to what you might be used to from "blocking" programming languages such as Java or Ruby. However, promises are compatible with the fast processing speed of the JavaScript event loop. Promises are also part of some object-data mappers in Node.js, such as Bookshelf (*http://bookshelfjs.org/*) or Serverbone (*http://serverbonejs.org/*).

There are currently a number of options for libraries to wrap asynchronous code execution with a promise on the server. We will take a closer look at the Bluebird library (*https://github.com/petkaantonov/bluebird*) by Petka Antonov.

Conceptually, a promise from the Movies data store works as follows. When an HTTP request GET /api/movies hits the server, the Movies data store will be called to provide the movie's data. Since loading data from a data store can take some time, the function ds.allMovies() returns a promise, which can resolve either to a success or failure, and you can switch the HTTP response depending on the promise outcome with then() and catch():

```
server.get('/api/movies', function (req, res, next) {
  return ds.allMovies()
      .then(function(m) { res.send(m); })
      .catch(function(err) { res.send(500, err) });
});
```

With this construct, data is sent to the client when the promise resolves, or an error is sent if there is a problem. For the purposes of illustration, the preceding response (which is written without promises) would look as follows with callbacks:

```
server.get('/api/movies', function (req, res, next) {
  ds.allMoviesCB(function(err, movies) {
    if (err) {
      res.send(500, err);
    }
    res.send(movies);
  });
});
```

An important difference to the promise style is, and this is again a matter of opinion, how exceptions are treated. With promises, you can mute an exception and control errors implicitly. While with callbacks, the Node process can "explode" and might not return a response to the client.

Next up, let's look at the implementation of a very basic data store in *DS.js*. First, we install Bluebird with npm:

```
$ npm install bluebird --save
```

Our data store first reads a file with JSON data. In Node.js, reading a file is also an asynchronous operation and a perfect use case for a promise.

To start, we bring in the dependencies into the data store *DS.js*, which are:

```
// We require the filesystem library first
var fs = require('fs');
var fileName = "./movies.json";
var _ = require('underscore');

// Next, we require the Promise library
var Promise = require('bluebird');
```

An important command from Bluebird is promisifyAll. With this command, you can obtain new functions with a suffix Async that wraps the original function in a promise. Because we will need operations from the filesystem, we do the following:

```
// We need to wrap the methods from the filesystem with:
Promise.promisifyAll(fs);
```

Next, we read the movies once into memory:

```
var Movies;

// prepare Data
var Movies = fs.readFileAsync(fileName, "utf8")
  .then(JSON.parse)
```

The idea here is to use the promise version of fs.readFile and parse the file into JSON objects. An important property of promises is chaining, and you will see how to add further operations later.

With this basic setup, we can build the "core" of a simple data store:

```
// map only ID and title of a movie
function _mapAttributes(movie) {
  return {
    id: movie.id,
    title: movie.title
  };
}

// map all movies attributes
function _mapAllAttributes(movie) {
  return {
    title: movie.title,
    description: movie.description,
```

```
    showtime: movie.showtime,
    rating: movie.rating,
    genres: movie.genres,
    _key: sha1(movie.title),
  };
}
// We will later export the data store to a module
var DS = function() {};

DS.prototype.allMovies = function() {
  allMovies: function() {
    return Movies.map(_mapAttributes)
  }
}
```

This is the most simple operation: listing all movies. With this, we *map* all movies from the `Movies` promise to a simplified JSON structure. In `_mapAttributes`, we just pick a simple primary key `id` and the title from the full movies data set. This mapping is an important part of a data "schema," and we will come back to the role of the `id` attribute in a second.

To get something running, you can export this basic module with:

```
module.exports = DS;
```

To see the basic schema in action, you can start a new API process with:

```
$ node api.js
```

And from the command line, we invoke the following test with `curl`:

```
$ curl 0.0.0.0:5001/api/movies | jshon
```

The output from the `curl` command is piped into `jshon`, a small command-line JSON beautifier.

We should obtain a result similar to:

```
[
  {
    "id": 13,
    "title": "The Twilight Saga: Eclipse"
  },
  {
    "id": 14,
    "title": "Mission: Impossible - Ghost Protocol"
  }
]
```

Similarly, you can build an API endpoint that finds a single movie resource. First, let's add a `find` function to *DS.js*:

```
function _find(movies, key) {
  var match = _.find(movies, function(movie) {
```

```
      return movie.id === parseInt(key)
    });
    if (!match) {
      throw Promise.RejectionError("ID not found");
    } else {
      return match;
    }
  }

  DS.prototype.find = function(key) {
    return Movies.then(function(movies) {
      return _find(movies, key);
    })
    .then(_mapAllAttributes);
  }
```

Note that the promise is rejected when no movie is found with a `Promise.Rejectio
nError`. This operation "error" can be caught from the *api.js* as follows:

```
server.get('/api/movies/:key', function(req, res, next) {
    return ds.find(req.params.key)
            .then(function(m) { res.send(m); })
            .error(function (e) {
              res.send(404, {err: e.message});
            })
            .catch(function(err) { res.send(500, err) });
});
```

To check that this works, you can do:

```
$ curl 0.0.0.0:5001/api/movies/12 | jshon

{
 "title": "The Artist",
 "description": "A silent movie star meets a young dancer, but
   the arrival of talking pictures sends their careers in
   opposite directions.",
 "showtime": 1388770080,
 "id": 12,
 "rating": 2,
 "genres": [
 "Drama",
 "Comedy"
 ],
 "director": "Michel Hazanavicius",
 "year": 2009
 }
```

With these basic endpoints, let's look again at the role of the data "schema," the blueprint
that defines how valid data should look like.

The role of the `id` attribute is especially important. Depending on the data store that
you use, there are different ways to represent the primary key:

- In many databases, particularly relational databases, primary keys often are in form of 1,2,3,…
- Many document stores use more complex IDs, because data can be distributed among different nodes, and strategies must be taken to prevent conflicts of IDs. So, we would be able to resolve IDs such as "7658095015."

To understand how we can control the mapping of primary keys to models in Backbone collection, let's experiment a bit. What if the primary key of the data store is not called *id* but *_key* instead? Let's simulate this scenario as follows in *DS.js*:

```
function _mapAttributes(movie) {
  return {
    title: movie.title,
    _key: sha1(movie.title),
  };
};
```

Now, we will use a SHA1 calculation to generate a custom primary key. For this, you can use the "SHA1" in the Node package and install it with:

```
$ npm install sha1 --save
```

When we now run a test with `curl`, we should see something like the following:

```
[
  {
    "_key": "3aa4e093a294c5a8ebef09a18a0d172d2c37a03b",
    "title": "X-Men: First Class"
  },
  {
    "_key": "6ee51f26282403baac57bd8affd19d9e67ab4252",
    "title": "Django Unchained"
  }
]
```

Because the _key attribute should be used to look up models, we adapt the show route to find method as follows:

```
var match = _.find(movies, function(movie) {
  return sha1(movie.title) === key
});
```

Let's play with this data store in the Backbone application for Munich Cinema. First, because the primary key of the data is not anymore mapped to `id`, but to _key, we must tell our Backbone model about the different setup.

Therefore, you must add the _key mapping in *app/models/movie.js*, as follows:

```
var Movie = Backbone.Model.extend({
  idAttribute: '_key'
```

```
  });
  return Movie;
```

The idAttribute tells a Backbone model to use a different mapping for fetching and updating models.

To test that this works, you can wire up fetching the details of a single movie in the router with:

```
routes: {
  'details/:key': 'showDetails'
},

showDetails: function(key) {
  var movie = new Movie({_key: key});
  this.listenTo(movie, 'all', function(ev) { console.log(ev) });
  movie.fetch();
}
```

If we load this route in the browser, you should see the request to the movies API using the _key attribute, as shown in Figure 8-1.

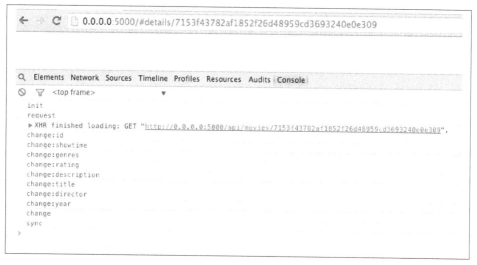

Figure 8-1. By using the idAttribute in a model, Backbone uses a different key when fetching a model

Let's continue with learning about persisting application state to the API—for example, to store votes on movies.

Persistence

Our goal is to let users provide a rating with "stars" for movies. For this, we track the average rating of a movie, as well as the votes of a user on a movie.

For voting, we define the following API endpoint:

```
PUT /movies/:key
parameters: vote
```

The idea is, after users vote on a movie, we calculate a new score on the server and respond with the average score for a movie.

Again, we start by setting up some logic on the backend for voting on movies. For the API in *api.js*, you can add the following route:

```
server.put("/api/movies/:key", function(req, res, next) {
    return ds.voteMovie(req.params.key, req.body.vote)
            .then(function(m) { res.send(m); })
            .error(function (e) {
              res.send(404, {err: e.message});
            })
            .catch(function(err) { res.send(500, err) });
});
```

And the new operation `voteMovie()` in the data store *./DS.js* looks like the following outline:

```
DS.prototype.voteMovie = function(id, vote, voter) {
  var that = this;
  return Movies
    .then(function() {
      return that.voteExists(id, 0)
    })
    .then(function(result) {
      return that.addVote(vote, id, voter)
    })
    .then(function() {
       return that.computeScore(id)
     })
    .then(function(score) {
       return that.updateScore(id, score);
    })
    .then(function() {
      return that.showMovie(id);
    });
  }
```

The basic promise chain is the following: check that users only vote once on a movie, add the vote, and compute a new score. As ranking algorithms can vary, the implementation of `computeScore` and `updateScore` is not treated in the book context. But you might want to take a look at the GitHub repo of the book for some ideas.

The new route can be tested via the API endpoints for the application simply with `curl`:

```
$ curl -X PUT \
     -d "{'vote': 1}" \
     0.0.0.0:5001/api/movies/26fc6f540d3a319b0d650df59e0df6ffa05a3224
```

And, as you can see, the `rating` attribute increases:

```
{
  "rating": 2,
  "description": "To control the oceans, Lord Cutler Beckett ..."
  "showtime": 1388733380,
  "title": "Pirates of the Caribbean: At World's End",
  "director": "Gore Verbinski",
  "_key": "26fc6f540d3a319b0d650df59e0df6ffa05a3224",
  "year": 2007,
  "genres": [
   "Action",
   "Adventure",
   "Fantasy"
  ],
  "length": 169
}
```

Now, to persist votes form the Backbone application, you can use the `save` function from Backbone. Similar to `fetch`, you can pass extra parameters via an options hash.

One simple way to send a vote to the API would be with the following Ajax request in *app/models/movie.js*:

```
voteMovie: function(stars) {
  var that = this;
  this.save({ type: "PUT",
           url: "/movies/" + this.id,
           contentType: 'application/json',
           data: JSON.stringify({vote: stars})
  })
  .then(function(movie) {
    that.set({rating: stars, score: movie.score, rank: movie.rank});
  })
  .fail(function(err) {
    console.log(err);
  });
}
```

When you now go to the browser and require this movie with:

```
var Movies = require('collections/movie');
movies = new Movies();
movie = movies.get(4);
movie.voteMovie(3);
```

the movie rating will be saved. In this simple example of saving a model, we don't require advanced validation logic that can be automatically triggered with Backbone. We will see an example of validating attributes before saving the next chapter, when we discuss the signup of a new user.

Conclusion

This chapter covered the basics of developing an API for a Backbone application. We used JavaScript and Restify to set up an API process, and we built a basic data store based on JavaScript promises. Next, we discussed the importance of mapping the primary key on the server to an ID attribute on the client side. Finally, we saw how to save the new state of a Backbone model to the server.

A voting application without protection of votes does not make much sense, however. We want users to sign up and sign in before they are allowed to submit votes. Also, the validation logic is important when storing data on the server. We'll work all this out in the next chapter, which covers how to use sessions to deal with multiple users and votes.

CHAPTER 9

Authentication

Many applications require spaces for public and private information. This often means two things: while interfaces should look different depending on who users are, server-side data must be protected from outsiders.

For example, users of the Munich Cinema application could store which movies they liked and maintain a history of favorite movies. They might also comment on other users' choices or maintain a personal calendar for movies to watch.

For all these actions, the application needs to know who we are (authentication), and what we are allowed to do (authorization). Authentication and authorization over HTTP are closely related.

In this chapter, our goal is to understand aspects of security in browsers and the backend requirements.

We will discuss the following:

- Security of Backbone applications
- Principles of client-server authentication
- Managing sessions
- Modal dialogs for signup and login

Security in Browsers

Bringing security to web browsers is a difficult task. Ideally, we want to authenticate every HTTP request. But practically, entering passwords multiple times can often become frustrating for users. Unfortunately, browsers do not provide native support for secure sessions right now, and most authentication strategies are vulnerable to attacks.

To solve the authentication dilemma over HTTP, there are basically two approaches:

Cookies

> This is the most popular, but also one of the less secure approaches to securing web applications in browsers. The main vulnerabilities of cookies are that they can be hijacked (e.g., with network sniffers) or stolen. Also, the content in cookies could be guessed by observing many of them. By putting random content in a cookie, this can be minimized, but it still can be a problem.

Signing requests

> When an HTTP request from the browser is made, a parameter in a URL, or in the HTTP header of the request, is sent along. This strategy goes under the name "signing" requests. Different signing strategies for requests exist, but the general advantage is the compatibility with RESTful principles. In contrast to cookies, we don't introduce a tight coupling between client and server. This is the most secure approach so far in web browsers, but also takes the most effort to implement.

Popular approaches for signing requests are basic auth and third-party authentication. With basic auth, a username and password are sent over the network with every request. Without using an SSL connection, basic auth is rather insecure, as attackers could see user credentials in plain text.

You should be aware of two common vulnerabilities of JavaScript applications: cross-site scripting (XSS) and cross-site request forgery (CSRF). While XSS vulnerabilities can especially occur if you allow users to submit content (such as in posts or comments in forums), CSRF is more subtle. By exploiting known links or settings in cookies, an attacker can potentially make HTTP requests on behalf of a user without her permission. Both approaches and security approaches with Backbone are described in Stephen A. Thomas's blog post "Securing Javascript Web Apps" (*http://blog.sathomas.me/post/securing-javascript-web-apps*).

Security is improved when your application uses OAuth tokens in HTTP headers. Users are redirected to an external OAuth provider, such as Twitter or Facebook, to obtain an access token for your application. Your web application can then use this token for signing requests.

However, authentication with cookies is the easiest type to understand. Once we understand the idea, we can replace cookie authentication with signing requests for OAuth. The following section discusses this approach in more depth.

Cookies

To give users a private space in the application, we need a sense of user identity on the client and on the server. We need to introduce the idea of state being "in use," or user sessions.

This conflicts a bit with HTTP, because HTTP is stateless, while user sessions introduce some "memory" to avoid multiple password inputs for each request.

HTTP cookies are a pragmatic solution to deal with this conflict. As can be seen in Figure 9-1, the client invokes a request to obtain the state of a session. To grant permissions to vote on a movie or display votes of the past, a session must be valid.

 Using cookies couples a browser to a server and is not very RESTful. According to RESTful principles, browsers don't have any state, and HTTP requests should be signed to conserve the addressability principle. For this, access tokens in an HTTP header or as a URL parameter are often used.

Cookies are stored in the browser until they expire. With every request from the client to the API, we check the cookies on the server side and compare whether a session is still valid. If not, a user needs to request a new cookie.

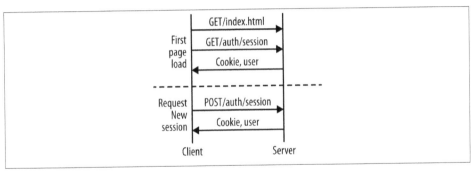

Figure 9-1. On first page load, we are interested in whether a user has a working session —we want to render the screen differently if he has (he can see his private information and can do more); if a user has not yet had a valid session, we need some way to provide one

Our basic authentication is the following: before users can request a session, they must register with the site. Once they have signed up, we need to have ways for users to manage a session—specifically, a check of whether a session is (still) valid, calls to obtain a new session, and finally, a call to delete a session or logout. For this, we will set up some new API endpoints.

These API calls will provide the background in this chapter, and we'll first discuss some possible implementations.

A word must be said on client-side versus server-side rendering of HTML in this context. With server-side rendering, it is possible to embed the state of a session in the first page load. For example, if a valid cookie has been sent in the first request, the server could respond with HTML where data on a user is embedded. The discussion for authentication with support of server-side rendering would be different.

Signup

To create new users on the server, we need to provide the following API endpoint:

```
POST /api/auth/create_user
This request allows to register a new user in the system. A user should provide
us with basic credentials. If a users signs up, we get a 200, if a username is
taken a 422 is returned, and for all other problems a 500
```

For user signup, you can add a new route to *api.js* and use a promise to wrap the database access ds.createUser(…) as follows:

```
server.post('/api/auth/create_user', function(req, res, next) {
  ds.createUser(req.body)
    .then(function(user) {
      res.send({id: user.id, username: user.username});
    })
    .error(function(err) {
      res.send(422, { error: err.message });
    })
    .catch(function(err) {
      res.send(500, { error: err });
    });
});
```

Before looking at the details of ds.createUser(…), have a look at the different paths that the promises can take:

- For the success path, the user is successfully created and we send back a user ID together with the user data. You could add information on authentication, such as a cookie or HTTP header, if you want to provide a direct login after signup.

- If a username is taken, the promise is rejected, and the Backbone application must process a 422 Unprocessable Entity (WebDAV; RFC 4918).

- When an unexpected error occurs, you send back a 500 (Internal Server Error) response, including an error message.

Now, let's look how the createUser method wraps the database access. To keep it simple, you can write the following implementation of createUser in the data store *DS.js*:

```
var Users = [];
function _createUser(raw) {
    var userId = Users.length + 1;
    var newUser = {
        id: userId,
        username: raw.username,
        password: raw.password,
        email: raw.email
    };

    // would require DB access
    Users.push(newUser);
    return _returnUser(newUser);
}
```

With the private function _createUser(), data would be stored in a data store. In our case, we just push the new user to the Users array. Next, we only want to return the user ID and username of a user:

```
function _returnUser(newUser) {
    return _.pick(newUser, 'username', 'id')
}
```

And last, before we actually create a user from an HTTP request, you should check for duplicates as follows:

```
function _findByUsername(username) {
    var user = _.findWhere(Users, {username: username});

    // _simulate_ a DB operation with time dependency
    return Promise.delay(30).thenReturn(user);
}

function _checkDuplicates(raw) {
    var username = raw.username;

    // would require DB access
    return _findByUsername(username).then(function(existingUser) {

        if (existingUser) {
            return Promise.RejectionError('Username taken.');
        }
        return raw;
    });
}
```

Now, the createUser function is as simple as:

```
DS.prototype.createUser = function(req) {
    var raw = JSON.parse(req.body);
    return _checkDuplicates(raw)
        .then(_createUser);
}
```

You can test the function with the following `curl` call:

```
$ curl -X POST 0.0.0.0:5001/api/auth/create_user \
    -H 'content-type: application/json' \
    -d '{"username": "beppo", "password": "pass", "email": "b@test.com"}'
```

And as response, you should see:

```
{"id":1}
```

If you run the same `curl` call again, you will see:

```
{"error":"Username taken."}
```

This error will be important later, when we add a validation to a Backbone user model. But we first continue with adding session management to the API.

Managing Sessions

Conceptually, when a user logs in, a cookie is set. Every request that follows carries this session information. For this, we need an API endpoint that sets up a cookie:

```
POST /api/auth/session
Setup a cookie if a user logs in with valid credentials
```

Sessions and cookies are easily confused. By definition, sessions persist until the user shuts down their browser. Cookies have an expire attribute and persist for a longer duration.

An important difference between session and cookie is that sessions can generally be trusted. Sessions are under control at the server, while information from a cookie can be manipulated or stolen.

 Cookie theft can be made more difficult by setting the `http-only` flag. For more details about this approach, consult Jeff Atwood's "Protecting Your Cookies: HttpOnly" (*http://www.codinghorror.com/blog/2008/08/protecting-your-cookies-httponly.html*).

To provide sessions in the Backbone application, we need two more API calls. One for checking if a session exists, and one endpoint for session logout:

```
POST /api/auth/session
Return basic user information, such as user ID and username, if a user
successfully enters her credentials. Return a 422 if either the username
or password is missing. Return a 403 if the password is wrong. Additionally,
an 'auth' attribute is returned to identify if a HTTP session was (not)
successfully initiated

GET /api/auth/session
Checks whether we have a valid session
```

```
DELETE /api/auth/session
Logout
```

Next, let's prepare the use of sessions for the Backbone app at the server side by extending the API. After a successful login, we set a cookie in the HTTP header with Set-Cookie.

For starting a user session, you want to validate the presence of user credentials only once. Therefore, you could start the route */api/auth/session* in *api.js* as follows:

```
server.post('/api/auth/session', function(req, res, next) {

  if (!req.body.username || !req.body.password) {
    res.send(422, {status: 'err',
      error: 'Username and password are two required fields.'
    });
    next();
  }

  ds.authUser(req)
    .then(function(activeUser) {
      res.header('Set-Cookie', 'session=' + activeUser.token
                + '; expires=Thu, 1 Aug 2030 20:00:00 UTC; path=/; HttpOnly');
      res.send({ auth: "OK", id: activeUser.id,
                username: activeUser.username,
                email: activeUser.email });
    })
    .error(function(err) {
      res.header('Set-Cookie', 'session=; HttpOnly')
      res.send(403, { auth: "NOK", error: err.message });
    })
    .catch(function(err) {
      console.log("/auth/session: %", err);
      res.send(401, { auth: "NOK" });
    })
});
```

As you can see, in case of the success path of the promise, an HTTP cookie is set. When the promise from ds.authUser is rejected, the HTTP cookie is cleared, and a 403 (Forbidden) response is generated.

What does the ds.authUser do? The authentication operations in ds.authUser will generally involve some database lookup and some code to compare hashes of passwords. We skip the details here, but you can see some more details on the book's GitHub page (*https://github.com/pipefishbook/pipefishbook.github.io*). For the Backbone app, it is important that a unique token can be attached to users from the data store *DS.js*:

```
// data store operations to authenticate a user
function _matchPasswords(req) {
  return _findByUsername(req.body.username).then(function(activeUser) {
    if (activeUser && req.body.password === activeUser.password) {
      return activeUser;
    } else {
```

```
          return Promise.RejectionError('username not found');
        }
      });
    }

    function _generateToken(activeUser) {
      var token = sha1(_.now().toString()); // generate a unique token
      activeUser.token = token;
      return activeUser;
    }
    DS.prototype.authUser = function(req) {
      return _matchPasswords(req).then(_generateToken);
    }
```

Also with `curl`, it is possible to activate a session as follows:

```
$ curl -v -X POST 0.0.0.0:5001/api/auth/session    \
        -H 'content-type: application/json'       \
        -c token.txt                              \
        -d '{"username": "beppo", "password": "pass"}'
```

And you should see a response similar to the following:

```
> POST /api/auth/session HTTP/1.1
> User-Agent: libcurl/7.21.4 OpenSSL/0.9.8r zlib/1.2.5
> Host: 0.0.0.0:5001
> Accept: application/json
> content-type: application/json
> Content-Length: 41
>
< HTTP/1.1 200 OK
< Set-Cookie: session=e48b670ee65a7fae0f61772172bebd2956b7ef5c;
<             expires=Thu, 1 Aug 2030 20:00:00 UTC; path=/; HttpOnly
< Content-Type: application/json
< Content-Length: 60
< Access-Control-Allow-Origin: *
< Access-Control-Allow-Headers: Accept, Accept-Version, Content-Length,
<           Content-MD5, Content-Type, Date, Api-Version, Response-Time
< Access-Control-Allow-Methods: POST
< Access-Control-Expose-Headers: Api-Version, Request-Id, Response-Time
< Connection: Keep-Alive
< Content-MD5: jdbl/l65DKaRSReguYM9IA==
< Date: Wed, 23 Apr 2014 19:17:13 GMT
< Server: api
< Request-Id: e0089060-cb1b-11e3-9ae3-6f4dd4cfa1a1
< Response-Time: 2
<
* Connection #0 to host 0.0.0.0 left intact
* Closing connection #0
{"auth":"OK","id":1,"username":"beppo","email":"b@test.com"}
```

Additionally, the `curl` command saved the cookie in a *token.txt* file that contains the following content:

```
# Netscape HTTP Cookie File
# http://curl.haxx.se/rfc/cookie_spec.html
# This file was generated by libcurl! Edit at your own risk.

#HttpOnly_0.0.0.0    FALSE / FALSE 1911844800 session  e48b670ee65a7fae0
```

Once a session is active, we need to validate a token against valid tokens from users. To do this, you add a function checkAuth in the data store *DS.js* as follows:

```
function _findUserByToken(req) {
  var cookies = getCookies(req);

var user = _.findWhere(Users, { token: cookies.session });

  // _simulate_ a DB operation with time dependency
  return Promise.delay(30).thenReturn(user);
}

DS.prototype.checkAuth: function(req) {
  return _findUserByToken(req).then(function(activeUser) {
    if (!activeUser) {
      return Promise.reject("No Session")
    }
    return _returnUser(activeUser);
  });
}
```

There is a helper needed to parse cookies. This parser can be added in a *lib* folder under *cookiesParser.js*:

```
var getCookies  = function(request) {
  var cookies = {};
  request.headers && request.headers.cookie &&
  request.headers.cookie.split(';').forEach(function(cookie) {
    var parts = cookie.match(/(.*?)=(.*)$/)
    cookies[ parts[1].trim() ] = (parts[2] || '').trim();
  });
  return cookies;
};
module.exports = getCookies;
```

Now, let's add an endpoint for GET /api/auth:

```
server.get('/api/auth/session', function(req, res, next) {
  ds.checkAuth(req)
    .then(function(user) {
      res.send({ auth: "OK", id: user.id, username: user.username });
    })
    .error(function(err) {
      res.header('Set-Cookie', 'session=; HttpOnly')
      res.send(403, { auth: "NOK", error: err.message });
    })
    .catch(function(err) {
      // error
      res.header('Set-Cookie', 'session=; HttpOnly')
```

```
      res.send(403, { auth: "NOK" });
  });
});
```

And again you can test the idea with `curl`:

```
$ curl -v 0.0.0.0:5001/api/auth/session -b token.txt

> GET /api/auth/session HTTP/1.1
> User-Agent: libcurl/7.21.4 OpenSSL/0.9.8r zlib/1.2.5
> Host: 0.0.0.0:5001
> Cookie: session=182b39c7347a587d584d92545a1f1dc341754871
> Accept: application/json
>
< HTTP/1.1 200 OK
< Content-Type: application/json
< Content-Length: 39
< Access-Control-Allow-Origin: *
< Access-Control-Allow-Headers: Accept, Accept-Version, Content-Length
< Access-Control-Allow-Methods: POST, GET
< Access-Control-Expose-Headers: Api-Version, Request-Id, Response-Time
< Connection: Keep-Alive
< Content-MD5: hIFmw2EZ305jVJGz0Gupog==
< Date: Wed, 23 Apr 2014 19:36:03 GMT
< Server: api
< Request-Id: 81b05040-cb1e-11e3-bb04-517baaa76d9b
< Response-Time: 2
<
* Connection #0 to host 0.0.0.0 left intact
* Closing connection #0
{"auth":"OK","id":1,"username":"beppo"}
```

Last, to reset a session, the DELETE `/api/auth` looks as follows:

```
server.del('/api/auth/session', function(req, res, next) {
  ds.clearSession(req)
  .then(function() {
    res.header('Set-Cookie', 'session=; HttpOnly')
    res.send(200, {auth: 'NOK'});
  });
});
```

The idea of clear session looks as follows:

```
DS.prototype.clearSession = function(req) {
  return _findUserByToken(req).then(function(activeUser) {
    if (activeUser) {
      activeUser.auth = null;
    }
    return activeUser;
  });
}
```

And if you verify the idea with `curl`, you can observer that all cookies will be gone:

```
$ curl -v -X DELETE 0.0.0.0:5001/api/auth/session -b token.txt
```

With these basic API endpoints for login, we continue to the corresponding Backbone actions on the client side.

Sessions with Backbone

On the client side, the API from the previous section allows us to build actions for sign up and sign in. Also, we can render views differently depending on the login state. For example, we might want to show different buttons in the header, and actions to "like" and "rate" movies, depending on whether a user is logged in.

So, let's prepare our UI to show forms for signup and login, as well as a dynamic header with some profile information.

A Navbar View

In most web applications, session management is taken care of on the top part of the screen with a navigation view or "navbar." In this view, you can render profile information and logout or login actions depending on the state of the user sessions.

As the navbar view manages views for signup and login, it is a kind of layout view on its own. Its rendering behavior is also different depending on whether users are logged in.

We can apply ideas to manage views as discussed in previous chapters and bind the view to a Session model and corresponding events for login and logout. Let's walk through the code of *app/views/navbar.js*:

```
var Backbone = require('backbone');
var _ = require('underscore');
var $ = Backbone.$;
var Handlebars = require('handlebars');
var Templates = require('templates/compiledTemplates')(Handlebars);

var LoginView = require('views/login');
var JoinView = require('views/join');
var Session = require('models/session');

var NavbarView = Backbone.View.extend({

    template: Templates['navbar'],
```

To set up the view, you require Backbone and dependencies for templating, as well as child views and a new Session model. This model will be used to talk to the API from earlier, and represents the state of a user session.

You only will need one Session instance per app, and the instance is setup in the constructor of the Navbar in *app/views/navbar.js*:

```
initialize: function() {
  // make sure to keep the layout reference from the callbacks
  _.bindAll(this, 'render', 'login', 'join', 'logout');

  // the navbar manages a session instance as will be discussed
  this.session = Session.getInstance();

  // instantiate the modals:
  this.loginView = new LoginView();
  this.joinView = new JoinView();

  // subscribe to events for login:
  this.listenTo(this.session, 'login:success', this.render);
  this.listenTo(this.session, 'logout:success', this.render);
}
```

This code makes sure that the this reference is set up correctly when callbacks for events are processed. The bindAll syntax from Underscore helps doing this. Then, you set up the Session model, the modal views for login/signup, and listen to events from the user session.

The session model decides how a Navbar is rendered, and what DOM events are bound to the view. In *app/views/navbar.js*, the following render function is used:

```
render: function() {
  var session = this.session.currentUser();
  this.$el.html(this.template({session: session}));
  if (session) {
    this.$el.delegate('.logout', 'click', this.logout);
  } else {
    this.$el.delegate('.login', 'click', this.login);
    this.$el.delegate('.join', 'click', this.join);
  }
  return this;
}
```

Because the events hash of a Navbar would be dynamic depending on the session state, you attach the event handlers manually with this.$el.delegate(…).

Last, you need some rendering logic when a user clicks on the DOM elements for login and signup. If a user wants to logout, no feedback is rendered. So, the view callbacks for DOM events in *app/views/navbar.js* could become:

```
// the modal for login is rendered here, as will be discussed:
login: function(ev) {
  ev.preventDefault();
  $('body').append(this.loginView.render().el);
},

// the modal for signup is rendered here, as will be discussed:
join: function(ev) {
  ev.preventDefault();
```

```
    $('body').append(this.joinView.render().el);
  },
  logout: function(ev) {
    ev.preventDefault();
    this.session.logout();
  },
```

Next, you can set up the template of the navbar view. In *app/templates/navbar.hbs*, you could define:

```
{{#if session }}
  <!-- active user session -->
  <a href="#" class="logout">Logout</a>
{{else}}
  <!-- no user session -->
  <a href="#" class="login">Login</a> |
  <a href="#" class="join">Join</a>
{{/if}}
```

Depending on the state in the session variable, you render the template differently: for active sessions, a user is able to logout. When no session is active, a user is able to log in or sign up.

The views for joining and login are modal boxes, so let's look at a base modal view next.

A Modal View for Sign Up

There are many different ways to design interfaces for signup, but a popular one is to break the application view with a modal dialog.

Because signup and login modal views are very similar, you can first write a modal base view in *app/views/modal.js*. Then, you customize the modal view behavior for the login and signup actions in *app/views/join.js* and *app/views/login.js*.

The base modal view is defined in *app/views/modal.js* as follows:

```
var Backbone = require('backbone');
var _ = require('underscore');
var $ = Backbone.$;

var ModalView = Backbone.View.extend({

  className: 'ui-modal',

  render: function() {
    this.$el.html(this.template());
    this.$el.delegate('.close', 'click', this.closeModal);
    this.$error = this.$el.find('.error');
    return this;
  },

  closeModal: function(ev) {
    if (ev) ev.preventDefault();
```

```
    this.$el.unbind();
    this.$el.empty();
    this.$el.remove();
  },

  initialize: function() {
    _.bindAll(this, 'render', 'closeModal');
    return Backbone.View.prototype.initialize.call(this);
  }

});
module.exports = ModalView;
```

Apart from adding a CSS class name ui-modal, there is logic to render and clean up the modal view. In particular, a modal view also manages an element for showing errors with this.$error.

We are now going to adapt the base modal view for the signup action. In *app/views/join.js*, you can inherit from the modal view as follows:

```
var Backbone = require('backbone');
var ModalView = require('views/modal');
var Handlebars = require('handlebars');
var Templates = require('templates/compiledTemplates')(Handlebars);
var $ = require('jquery-untouched');
var _ = require('underscore');

var User = require('models/user');

var JoinView = ModalView.extend({

template: Templates['join'],

events: {
  'submit': 'registerUser'
},

render: function() {
  ModalView.prototype.render.call(this);
  this.delegateEvents();
  return this;
},

registerUser: function(ev) {
  ev.preventDefault();
  this.user.clear();
  var username = $('input[name=username]').val();
  var password = $('input[name=password]').val();
  var email = $('input[name=email]').val();

  this.user.signup({username: username, password: password, email: email});
},

initialize: function() {
  this.user = new User();
```

```
        return ModalView.prototype.initialize.call(this);
    }
});
module.exports = JoinView;
```

As you can see from this code, the JoinView inherits from ModalView and extends the logic of initialize and render to account for custom events of JoinView. The regis terUser takes the values from the signup form and passes the values to a User model. How the User instance makes the API calls will be discussed in the next section.

To complete the UI for signup, you need to include a template and add some styling. In *app/templates/join.hbs*, you can add the following signup form:

```
<div class="overlay"></div>
<div class="content">
    <span class="close">close</span>
    <section class="join">
      <h1>Register</h1>
      <div class="error"></div>
      <form>
      <label for="username">Username</label>
      <input type="text" name="username" />
      <br>
      <label for="email">Email Address</label>
      <input type="text" name="email" />
      <br>
      <label for="password">Password</label>
      <input type="password" name="password" />
      <br>
      <input type="submit"></input>
    </section>
</div>
```

So far, the signup form template and view can pick up data from a user. Because the user data should be subsequently passed to the application backend, let's look at the data handling of *app/models/user.js* next:

```
var Backbone = require('backbone');
var _ = require('underscore');

var UserModel = Backbone.Model.extend({
    defaults: {
      username: '',
      password: '',
      email: ''
    },

urlRoot: '/api/auth/create_user',

validate: function(attrs) {
  var errors = this.errors = {};
  if (!attrs.username) errors.firstname = 'username is required';
  if (!attrs.email) errors.email = 'email is required';
```

```
      if (!_.isEmpty(errors)) return errors;
    },

    signup: function(attrs) {
      var that = this;
      this.save(attrs, {success: function(model, response) {
          that.trigger('signup:success');
        },
        error: function(model, response) {
          var error = JSON.parse(response.responseText).error;
          that.validationError = {"username": error};
          that.trigger('invalid', that);
        }
      });
    },

    save: function(attrs, options) {
      options || (options = {});

    options.contentType = 'application/json';
    options.data = JSON.stringify(attrs);

        return Backbone.Model.prototype.save.call(this, attrs, options);
      }
  });

  module.exports = UserModel;
```

A number of ideas are important here:

- To synch a `UserModel` with a server, we reference the `create_user` path from the API with the `urlRoot` property.

- The `UserModel` includes some validation logic of a Backbone model. Validating the user data is important to make sure that a user has entered all required fields in the form.

- The `signup` function wraps the `save` function of a Backbone model. This allows you to process errors that are coming from the server.

- The behavior of the `save` function is extended to pass JSON instead of text values to the server.

To improve the signup form, you can add some behavior for rendering errors in *app/ views/join.js*:

```
    renderError: function(err, options) {
      var errors = _.map(_.keys(err.validationError), function(key) {
        return err.validationError[key];
      })
      this.$error.text(errors);
    },
```

```
renderThanks: function() {
    this.$el.find('.join').html('thanks for signup');
}
```

And bind these callbacks to the invalid events in the constructor of *app/views/join.js*:

```
this.listenTo(this.user, 'invalid', this.renderError);
this.listenTo(this.user, 'signup:success', this.renderThanks);
```

A working signup form should then render feedback on a successful signup or about possible problems, as shown in Figure 9-2.

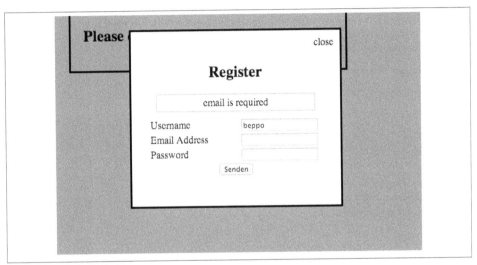

Figure 9-2. The view for signup is a custom modal view and handles errors from the validation of the UserModel

The Login Dialog

Similar to the modal view for signup, you can continue with a view for the login. Let's start with a template in *app/templates/join.js* this time:

```
<div class="overlay"></div>
  <div class="content">
  <span class="close">close</span>
  <h2>Login</h2>
  <div class="error"></div>
  <form id="login">
    <label for="username">
      Username:
    </label>
    <input name="username" />
    <br>
    <label for="password">
```

```
      Password:
    </label>
    <input type="password" name="password" />
    <br>
    <input type="submit"></input>
  </form>
</div>
```

This can be wired up to a modal dialog similar to the registration form. In *app/views/login.js*, you can add:

```javascript
var ModalView = require('views/modal');
var Handlebars = require('handlebars');
var Templates = require('templates/compiledTemplates')(Handlebars);
var $ = require('jquery-untouched');
var _ = require('underscore');

var Session = require('models/session');

var LoginView = ModalView.extend({

  template: Templates['login'],

  events: {
    'submit': 'login'
  },

  render: function() {
    ModalView.prototype.render.call(this);
    this.delegateEvents();
    this.$error = this.$el.find('.error');
    return this;
  },

  login: function(ev) {
    ev.preventDefault();
    var username = $('input[name=username]').val();
    var password = $('input[name=password]').val();

    // ... login action
    var that = this;
    Session.getInstance().login(username, password);
  },

  initialize: function() {
    this.session = Session.getInstance();
    this.listenTo(this.session, 'login:success', this.closeModal);
    return ModalView.prototype.initialize.call(this);
  }
});
module.exports = LoginView;
```

In contrast to the view for signup, the `LoginView` directly manages the user session with a `Session` instance. How the state of a session is tracked will be discussed in the next section. Let's continue first with working on the view for activating a session.

The Session Logic

Now that we have a user interface for creating sessions, let's continue with the logic to activate a user model.

A New Session

For login, all we need to do is fetch a cookie from the server. You can call the authentication API directly from the Session model in *app/models/session.js*:

```
login: function(username, password) {
    var that = this;
    var credentials = JSON.stringify({username: username,
                                      password: password });
    $.ajax({type: 'POST', dataType: 'json',
        contentType: "application/json",
        url: "/api/auth/session",
        data: credentials})
      .done(function(data) {
        that.user = new User(data);
        that.trigger('login:success');
      })
      .fail(function(response) {
        var error = JSON.parse(response.responseText).error;
        console.log(error);
        that.validationError = {"username": error};
        that.trigger('invalid', that);
    });
}
```

The paths through the promises can handle a successful login or the error from a failed login. In the case that our server responds with a "successful" authentication, we also set the user data from the backend.

State of a Session

Addtionally, there must be some logic to get the current state of a session in *app/models/session.js*. Often, this also means we will need to retrieve some information about the user.

A simple check whether we have a valid user session might be:

```
currentUser: function() {
    // ... retrieve currentUser if authenticated
    if (this.user && (this.user.get('auth') == 'OK')) {
      return this.user;
    } else {
      return false;
    }
}
```

First, we check if there is a user. Then, we check if the user hasn't logged out by retrieving the `auth` attribute.

Still, we have a problem. When the user reloads the page or visits the page on the next day, we might want to check in the background for a valid cookie. As long as we work with a static HTML, we need to process an extra API call.

So far we haven't used the `Session` model's `fetch` function so we can do it now as follows in *app/models/session.js*:

```
var deferred = this.fetch();
var self = this;
deferred.done(function(data) {
  self.user = new User(data);
});
deferred.fail(function() {
  self.user = null;
});
```

Now, we have enough logic to start personal conversations with users. We still need some logic to log out.

Logout

Technically, the logout should do the inverse of the login. That means killing a cookie and removing the session from the server:

```
logout: function() {
  // ... delete a session
  var that = this;
  $.ajax({type: 'DELETE', dataType: 'json',
    contentType: 'application/json',
    url: '/api/auth/session' })
      .done(function(data) {
        that.user.set('auth', 'NOK');
        that.trigger('logout:success');
      })
}
```

Conclusion

This chapter started out with some conceptual work needed to create security in web browsers. Cookies provide a pragmatic solution to make HTTP sessions safe and give a good foundation for exploring further authentication work. You saw a number of HTTP requests with `curl` to experiment with authentication from the command line.

We then built a user interface that allows users to sign up and log in. These views are based on a common modal view. The `JoinView` manages a `UserModel`, while the `Login View` manages a `Session` model, where the state of a session can be resolved.

With these new routes for authentication, you could go ahead and add more functions to voting on movies or maybe commenting. Because the application is evolving more and more into a full, single-page web application, a look at frameworks on top of Backbone might become interesting to you. To prepare you for using a Backbone framework, we will discuss workflow automation in the next chapter.

CHAPTER 10

Automated Workflows

As your application grows and you start working as a team with multiple developers, questions on workflow, coding style, and testing become important. Tools to organize workflows help to apply conventions and bring applications to the next level.

In this chapter, we enter the world of Yeoman. Based on the ideas of build automation, this chapter shows how a Yeoman generator can provide you with standard steps to develop Backbone application modules.

Bundled with Yeoman generators, there often comes a setup that favors the RequireJS module format over CommonJS modules. While CommonJS and Browserify are interesting when the JavaScript application must be loaded up front, RequireJS has its benefits if you are building a web application where parts of the experience should be loaded asynchronously as needed.

At the end of this chapter, our goal is to have the movie application running on the Node toolchains. This includes:

- How to fetch Backbone dependencies such as plug-ins using Bower
- Yeoman and a Backbone generator, which will help scaffolding project structures
- Using RequireJS for development
- Using a build with RequireJS project

Improving Productivity

In the previous chapters, you incrementally have built a web application "by hand." This means that you ran commands from the command line to create files and directories, inserted repeating code by hand, and maybe applied a watchmode of different tools to help establish the development environment.

If you work on different projects or on a team with several developers, it can be helpful to work with certain "default" project configurations. Generators for project components are an important building block of some frameworks on top of Backbone, too, such as the Thorax generator (which will be discussed in Chapter 11).

Most tools for workflow automation are actually framework agnostic, but a number of tools are repeatedly discussed in the Backbone ecosystem:

Yeoman (http://yeoman.io/)
> With Yeoman generators, you can easily scaffold Backbone projects and components to avoid "boring" steps, such as creating directories and files. Many Yeoman generators provide support for a build process based on Grunt or Gulp. With this combination, your team gets some extra support not only to develop and test web applications with Backbone, but also to make an application production ready.

Brunch (https://github.com/brunch/brunch)
> Brunch is a very popular choice for building applications with the Chaplin framework. With it, you can easily create a project skeleton of a Backbone application. Also, Brunch supports a watch mode during application development, compilation of CoffeeScript to JavaScript, and a deploy function.

Catero (https://github.com/rotundasoftware/cartero)
> Cartero offers a management system for growing projects based on Browserify and CommonJS. With it, you can bundle your JavaScript together with CSS and HTML such that they become easier to reuse across different or one large frontend project.

Because tools for automating workflows and project builds make choices for you, it can be important to study in detail how it will affect your application. For example, if you decide to use a Yeoman generator—as we will explore in this chapter—it might affect the way your application dependencies are managed or how your JavaScript application is built.

As many frontend communities are adopting Yeoman and RequireJS, the overview of this chapter hopefully can make you understand the implications. However, this chapter marks a brief departure from the example application used in previous chapters. So, it is best to start in a clean directory.

Dependencies with Bower

In contrast to full stack JavaScript developers, the preferred way of many frontend developers to manage dependencies is given by Bower (*http://bower.io/*). When you generate a project with Yeoman, a bower dependency is often included.

Similar to npm, Bower can help you locate and download required libraries in the right version. Bower has the advantage of not imposing a JavaScript module format. But on the other hand, with Bower, you will need to manage dependencies for the backend of your application separately as we did earlier with npm.

To install Bower, use the following:

```
$ npm install -g bower
```

Next, you can initialize a new project with:

```
$ bower init
```

Then, we can either predefine libraries in the *bower.json* file, or manually run the bower install command. For example:

```
$ bower install jquery-mockjax
```

 With jquery-mockjax, you can easily mock data for browser development. If you just want to focus on browser development without exploring API requirements, jquery-mockjax might be a good alternative to a canned setup.

Also, you could install the Backbone.Obscura plug-in from Chapter 7 with Bower as follows:

```
$ bower install backbone.obscura
```

When scaffolding a project with Yeoman, you will get a default *bower.json* file, where Backbone and its dependencies are already predefined. You then just need to add new plug-ins into the *bower.json* file and run the bower install again. Unfortunately, not all packages support the bower fetch process, as not all frontend JavaScript libraries support a certain module format. So, sometimes you still need to clone a Git repository and/or copy dependencies manually into a project.

Because Bower fetches the whole history of a dependency, it can be interesting to just copy over the actual JavaScript library into the application. For example, if you work with a hybrid JavaScript application stack, it can be interesting to track only referenced JavaScript libraries in the project repository. This can be done with bower-installer, which supports copying files from the */bower_components* directory:

```
$ npm -g install bower-installer
```

Then, you can add an install path to the *bower.json* file:

```
"install" : {
        "path" : "./js/libs"
  }
```

And then you run:

```
$ bower-installer
Setting up install paths...Finished
```

```
Running bower install...Finished
Installing:
   backbone.obscura : ./js/libs/backbone.obscura/backbone.obscura.js
   backbone : /Users/pmu/movies_node/./js/libs/backbone/backbone.js
   underscore : /Users/movies_node/./js/libs/underscore/underscore.js
   jquery : /Users/pmu/movies_node/./js/libs/jquery/jquery.js
```

In the next section, we look at how Yeoman integrates Bower to manage dependencies in a Backbone project.

Say Hello to Yeoman

With `browserify` and Grunt, you have already had some experience with tools that automate steps in JavaScript development. We still may face some problems that come with growing applications, however. For example, how can we set up a new project from scratch? And how can we organize code in different directories?

Developers have different biases toward these question, but a number of themes are heard often:

- In development mode, projects should be loaded dynamically. Also, it must be possible to load components for tests. For this, some developers set up a watch mode to rebuild an application automatically after a change. We explored this idea with Grunt and `watchify` previously. But with RequireJS you get an additional option.
- So far, we organized code into directories /*models*, /*collections*, and /*views*. We also had to create a place for templates. The way we organize our files has quite some influence on how scalable our application becomes.

Instead of reinventing the wheel, we can look at the workflows from other developers. Because most workflow problems revolve around file management, let's look at Yeoman and the "generator" for Backbone.

Yeoman can create, fetch, and copy files according to conventions that are set in the generator that we specify. What this means will become clear in a moment.

First, you need to install Yeoman:

```
$ npm -g install yo
```

This will take a few minutes, depending on your network speed.

Next, run the following:

```
$ yo
```

This will return a small menu:

```
[?] What would you like to do?
    --------
```

```
      Update your generators
  〉 Install a generator
```

There are many different generators that define your project layout as well as dependencies in *package.json*, *bower.json*, and tasks in the Gruntfile. Because this is a Backbone book, we directly jump into the Backbone generator with:

```
npm install -g generator-backbone
```

Now we can run the Yeoman generator with:

```
$ yo backbone movies
```

The generator will ask some question about whether to include support for other kinds of frontend tools.

As a result, we should see a similar output:

```
      _-----_
     |       |
     |--(o)--|    .--------------------------.
     `---------´  |    Welcome to Yeoman,    |
     ( _´U`_ )    |   ladies and gentlemen!  |
     /___A___\    '_____'
      |  ~  |
    __'.___.'__
  ´   `  |° ´ Y `

Out of the box I include HTML5 Boilerplate, jQuery, Backbone.js and Modernizr.
[?] What more would you like?
 ○ Twitter Bootstrap for Sass
〉○ Use CoffeeScript
```

As our goal is project organization of Backbone applications, we only activate support for RequireJS. Then we should see that Yeoman builds our empty project:

```
create .bowerrc
create bower.json
create .jshintrc
create .editorconfig
create Gruntfile.js
create package.json
create app/styles/main.css
create app/404.html
create app/favicon.ico
create app/robots.txt
create app/.htaccess
create app/index.html
create app/scripts/main.js
invoke   mocha:app
create      test/index.html
create      test/lib/chai.js
create      test/lib/expect.js
create      test/lib/mocha/mocha.css
```

```
    create        test/lib/mocha/mocha.js
    create        test/spec/test.js
```

Yeoman will also go on with installing the projects dependencies under */node_modules*.

In our project directory, we now have *bower.json* and *package.json* files as well as a Gruntfile.

Let's explore the application directory from the Yeoman Backbone generator:

```
app
|-bower_components
|-images
|-scripts
|---collections
|---models
|---routes
|---templates
|---vendor
|---views
|-styles
```

We also got a file *main.js*—an important component for using RequireJS, which we will discuss in the next section—and directories for styles and testing.

Besides scaffoling a new project, the Backbone generator of Yeoman supports scaffolding Backbone views, routers, models, and collections. Scaffolding those files is not every developer's cup of tea, but it can help when you work in a RequireJS environment, as discussed in the next section.

For example, to scaffold a Movies router, you could run:

```
$ yo backbone:router movies
   create app/scripts/routes/movies.js
```

When you open the newly created router, you can already see the encapsulation based on RequireJS. Let's explore what this means.

RequireJS

Compared to working on a project based on npm and browserify, RequireJS provides an alternative to break up large components into smaller JavaScript files. This is based on the so-called AMD module format, where you "define" how dependencies must be loaded for each file. Because the way dependencies are resolved may differ between development and production environments, RequireJS supports a development mode and a build mode. Be sure to run the RequireJS early on to prevent problems with asynchronously loading external JavaScript libraries, such as maps.

Main.js

First, we need to discuss the *main.js* file. To resolve files and dependencies in a JavaScript application, RequireJS needs a mapping of the dependencies to URL paths. We define this mapping in *main.js* and also define the initial dependencies when an application is first loaded.

In our *main.js* that we have from the Yeoman generator, we already get Backbone.js configured and its dependencies included by default.

Inspecting the contents of *main.js*, we quickly can identify new keywords. For example, in the `require.config` part, we set up the global configuration of the modules and put dependencies that come from other libraries. In the *main.js* obtained from Yeoman, this looks like:

```
/*global require*/
'use strict';

require.config({
    shim: {
        underscore: {
            exports: '_'
        },
        backbone: {
            deps: [
                'underscore',
                'jquery'
            ],
            exports: 'Backbone'
        }
    },
    paths: {
        jquery: '../bower_components/jquery/jquery',
        backbone: '../bower_components/backbone/backbone',
        underscore: '../bower_components/underscore/underscore'
    }
});

require([
    'backbone'
], function (Backbone) {
    Backbone.history.start();
});
```

The main idea here is that we map files via `paths` to module references that we can use later in the application. We need this manual mapping, because not all libraries follow the AMD convention to declare their dependencies up front. So, we need to provide a `shim` that provides a depencency tree that RequireJS can resolve. If we add new libraries, we add a path and a shim. We later will see how to do this in the context of Backbone plug-ins.

Going to the *index.html* from Yeoman, we see a reference to *main.js*. Here, loading of modules happens when the browser parses the *index.html*:

```
<!-- build:js scripts/main.js -->
<script data-main="scripts/main" src="bower_components/requirejs/require.js">
</script>
<!-- endbuild -->
```

With this environment set up, we directly can start building the application.

Adding Modules

Assuming you used Yeoman to scaffold a router, you can rewrite the previous router example into AMD format as follows:

```
/*global define*/

define([
    'jquery',
    'backbone',
    'obscura',
    'collections/movies',
    'views/layout',
    'views/moviesList',
    'views/chose',
    'views/genres',
    'views/sort',
], function ($, Backbone, Obscura, Movies, Layout,
            MoviesList, ChoseView, GenresView, SortView ) {

    'use strict';

    var layout,
        movies,
        proxy,
        sortView,
        genresView,
        deferred;

    if (!proxy) {
      movies = new Movies();
      proxy = new Obscura(movies);
      deferred = movies.fetch();
    }

    var MoviesRouter = Backbone.Router.extend({
        routes: {
          "movies/:id":  "selectMovie",
          "":            "main"
        },

        main: function() {
```

```
        // ...
      },

      selectMovie: function(id) {
        // ...
      }

    });

    return MoviesRouter;
  });
```

The code is not much different from earlier, except that we wrap the code in a module by using `define`, declaring dependencies and lastly returning the module. Our `Movie sRouter` module requires all the sub pieces to return the wirings as a new module. Now, whenever we `depend` on the router, we include automatically the sub pieces. With RequireJS, we try to create smaller view and model pieces that only ask for the modular bits they need.

Scaffolding Components

With the Yeoman generator, you can add modules for the user interface from the command line with:

```
$ yo backbone:view layout
$ yo backbone:view movieList
$ yo backbone:view movie
...
```

And you need to generate modules for the data layer, too:

```
$ yo backbone:model genre
$ yo backbone:collection genres
$ yo backbone:model movie
$ yo backbone:collection movies
```

From these commands, we will obtain a bunch of Backbone views and collections. While wiring these files up similarly as you did in the earlier chapters, you will see that the RequireJS build system can resolve dependencies dynamically during development.

Also, with support from Grunt, you can again use different approaches for view templates, such as JST templates or Handlebars.

Conclusion

This chapter covered application development with an automated workflow based on Bower, Grunt, Yeoman, and RequireJS. The workflow automation comes at a price of learning new tools and having some more boilerplate in the JavaScript modules. However, because the future standard of JavaScript will evolve ways that support the AMD style of importing modules, you should have obtained some good foundations in this chapter.

Because build tools and generators play part in some JavaScript frameworks on top of Backbone, you will see how to apply the Yeoman generator from Thorax in the next chapter. Thorax supports an application stack that integrates Backbone and Handlebars and comes with a number of view helpers that simplify building large Backbone applications.

CHAPTER 11

From Backbone To Thorax

By now, the user interface of Munich Cinema has taken shape. You have used a number of patterns and plug-ins to build applications with Backbone.js. To simplify the way we manage JavaScript projects, we also saw different automations of programming tasks with Grunt and Yeoman. As a last step, let's look at a framework on top of Backbone.js where a number of previous ideas come together.

Authored by Ryan Eastridge and Kevin Decker, Thorax.js is an open source framework on top of Backbone.js that combines Backbone with Handlebars and some additional helpers. Thorax.js was optimized for mobile application but is increasingly used for single-page web applications as an alternative to Ember or Angular. With the Thorax.js generator, you get a tool for workflow automation. Also, Thorax comes with a Layout view, a CollectionView, and advanced event management out of the box.

This chapter might be interesting for you too, if you want to learn more about the Handlebars.js templating approach and view helpers.

In overview, we tackle the following topics:

- Productivity and scalability of an application
- Using Thorax for better view rendering
- Advanced interactions to select a movie

The Role of Frameworks

The philosophy of Backbone.js is based on simplicity and flexibility. As such, Backbone provides only a set of very basic components, such as views and collections.

While these components can be customized into any direction, we often start repeating a number of choices over and over. What we want in many situations are a number of blueprints that help us to make faster choices. This is especially useful if you regularly build new applications, or if your team has to maintain multiple projects.

Although frameworks help you with making development faster and easier, they often enforce a higher coupling between your business logic and implementing technology. In other words, if the framework changes, your application might need quite a few changes, too.

In the Backbone.js ecosystem, a number of frameworks exist:

Marionette (http://marionettejs.com/)
> This framework by Derick Bailey provides components to render collections to combine multiple views and boilerplate to manage events from different parts of an application. Marionette is one of the more popular frameworks on top of Backbone.js.

Thorax (http://thoraxjs.org/)
> Thorax combines the Handlebars.js templating approach with Backbone.js. As such, there are a number of view helpers that simplify the construction views. Additionally, Thorax supports improved data binding. Thorax also comes with a Yeoman generator for workflow automation.

Giraffe (http://barc.github.io/backbone.giraffe/)
> Giraffe was created by the team behind Barc, a widget to embed chats in a web application. The framework is very lightweight and provides a number of enhancements to manage events from the router or views. In Giraffe.Contrib, there are also a number of view components like a collection view.

Chaplin (http://chaplinjs.org/)
> Chaplin introduces a predefined structure on top of Backbone.js applications, supported by components such as ModelView, Controller, mediator, and Application. The Chaplin documentation (*http://docs.chaplinjs.org/*) illustrates how the components relate to one another.

Rendr (https://github.com/rendrjs/rendr)
> Rendr is a so-called isomorphic JavaScript framework, which looks somewhat similar to Thorax. The big difference, however, is that Rendr supports both server-side and client-side rendering, validation, and helper functions.

Junior (http://justspamjustin.github.io/junior/#home)
> Junior integrates helpers for views and the router that are optimized for building mobile applications. This framework is not only about JavaScript, but also provides CSS support for UI widgets.

Besides the direct usage of building applications faster, frameworks are also a good source for inspiration and developing an advanced understanding of Backbone.js techniques.

Measured in revenues of a Backbone.js web application, Walmart's shopping cart is among the largest Backbone applications around. This makes it interesting to look closer at Thorax.js.

In the following sections, you will learn some ways how Thorax.js provides a way toward mobile and single-page web applications.

Getting Started

Thorax comes out of the box with workflow automation based on Grunt, Yeoman, and Bower. As was discussed in Chapter 10, we can use Yeoman and install a generator that supports us creating applications with Thorax.

To install the Thorax generator, we run the following:

```
$ npm install -g generator-thorax
```

Next, we can scaffold a Thorax application with:

```
$ yo thorax cinema
```

You will be asked whether to use the "Chef's Choice" application stack. This is another name for *convention-over-configuration*. With this we mean a set of default configuration options that proved helpful for others. We happily answer "yes" and you can watch the dependencies getting installed. The main result of this is obtaining a directory structure, some dependencies, and a Gruntfile. Now, we are ready to go.

First, the Gruntfile of Thorax comes with a number of options for build tasks. The tasks are nicely distributed over files in the */tasks* directory, such that you can easily adapt the tasks to your personal setup:

```
styles.js
open-browser.js
ensure-installed.js
options
|
| watch.js
| thorax.js
| sass.js
| requirejs.js
| mocha_phantomjs.js
| karma.js
| jshint.js
| cssmin.js
| clean.js
| connect.js
| copy.js
```

Thorax comes with very good support for testing, too. The scope of this book does not include testing, but the reader is advised to look at the book *Backbone.js Testing* by Ryan Roemer to get a good introduction. *JavaScript Testing Recipes* (*http://jstesting.jcoglan.com/*) by James Coglan is also a good resource.

Apart from the Gruntfile and build tasks, we get support for Require.js, a *bower.json* file, and some basic project directory structure. However, we also get some support for Thorax-specific components. Let's have a look into *main.js*, where we manage the JavaScript dependencies:

```
require.config({
    deps: ['main'],
    paths: {
        'jquery': pathPrefix + 'bower_components/jquery/jquery',
        'underscore': pathPrefix + 'bower_components/underscore/underscore',
        'handlebars': pathPrefix + 'bower_components/handlebars/handlebars',
        'backbone': pathPrefix + 'bower_components/backbone/backbone',
        'thorax': pathPrefix + 'bower_components/thorax/thorax',
        'coffee-script': pathPrefix + 'bower_components/coffee-script/index',
        'cs': pathPrefix + 'bower_components/require-cs/cs',
        'text': pathPrefix + 'bower_components/text/text',
        'hbs': pathPrefix + 'bower_components/requirejs-hbs/hbs',
        'obscura': pathPrefix + "bower_components/backbone.obscura/backbone.obscura"
    },
    shim: {
        'handlebars': {
            exports: 'Handlebars'
        },
        'backbone': {
            exports: 'Backbone',
            deps: ['jquery', 'underscore']
        },
        'underscore': {
            exports: '_'
        },
        'thorax': {
            exports: 'Thorax',
            deps: ['handlebars', 'backbone']
        }
    }
});
```

By scanning the dependencies, you will see handlebars, the approach for templating in Thorax. We will discuss this in a moment, but let's first prepare again a sandbox for mock data.

Prepare Mock Data

As in the previous chapters, we want to work with some data mocks first. In a setup with RequireJS, you can use Mockjax (*https://github.com/appendto/jquery-mockjax*) and include it in the Bower file with:

```
$ bower install jquery-mockjax
```

and run:

```
$ bower install
```

In a *js/mocks.js* file, we include:

```
define(['jquery', 'mockjax'], function($) {

'use strict';

var mock = function() {
$.ajaxSetup({
  dataType: 'json'
});

  $.mockjax({
      url: '/api/movies',
      dataType: 'json',
      proxy: 'json/movies.json'
  });
};

  return {
    start: mock
  };
});
```

To later use the mock setup in the application, we need to provide a reference in *require-config.js*. Note that we have different RequireJS setups for development and production. Right now, we just set up the runtime dependencies for development:

```
'mockjax': pathPrefix + 'bower_components/jquery-mockjax/jquery.mockjax'

// shims
'mockjax': {
    deps: ['jquery']
}
```

As previously, we create mock data in *json/movies.json*:

```
[
 {
  "id": 12,
  "showtime": 1388770080,
  "genres": [
   "Drama",
   "Comedy"
```

```
  ],
  "rating": 0,
  "description": "A silent movie star meets a young dancer, ...",
  "title": "The Artist",
  "director": "Michel Hazanavicius",
  "year": 2009
},
{
  "id": 5,
  "showtime": 1388700300,
  "rating": 0,
  "description": "The film is set in New York, shortly after ...",
  "title": "Taxi Driver",
  "genres": [
    "Drama",
    "Action"
  ],
  "director": "Martin Scorsese",
  "year": 1974
},
]
```

and some data for genres in *json/genres.json*:

```
[
  {
    "id": 1,
    "name": "Drama",
    "count": 5
  },
  {
    "id": 2,
    "name": "Comedy",
    "count": 3
  },
  {
    "id": 3,
    "name": "Action",
    "count": 6
  }
]
```

Let's start building the application next.

Initializing the Application

As discussed in Chapter 4, the movies browser will be the main entry point to the application, and you can scaffold a router with Yeoman as follows:

```
$ yo thorax:router browser
```

The application template from the Thorax project generator comes with a `Hello World` router, so you must replace that router with the new browser by inserting the following into the *js/main.js* file:

```
require([
  'jquery',
  'backbone',
  'views/root',
  'routers/browser',
  'helpers',
], function ($, Backbone, RootView, Browser) {

initialize(function(next) {
  var browser = new Browser();

  next();
});

function initialize(complete) {
  $(function() {
    Backbone.history.start({
      pushState: false,
      root: '/',
      silent: true
    });

RootView.getInstance(document.body);

    complete(function() {
      Backbone.history.loadUrl();
    });
  });
}
});
```

The important idea is to resolve the root view and start rendering the views hierarchy.

To get a better feeling for the events on the main view, you might want to add the following for the development of the application:

```
var root = RootView.getInstance(document.body);
root.on("all", function(ev) { console.log(ev) });
```

We then see these events:

```
change:view:start
activated
child
change:view:end
```

Apart from adding the logger for events to trace certain commands, Thorax provides a global `Thorax` module, from where you can inspect instances of Thorax components. For example, you can grab all view classes when you run this in the browser console:

```
> T = require('thorax')
> Views = T.Views
```

So far, there are no child views and no other views that can be activated. To do this, let's continue building the router from where we set up the main application.

A Router Setup

For building the router, the setup from the Thorax generator is a good start. We can "borrow" ideas from the scaffolded setup in the HelloWorldRouter. As before, the task of the movies browser will be to show lists and details of movies. And as a start, you can add routes for the list of movies and the movies details. This results in:

```
define([
  'backbone',
  'mocks'
], function (Backbone, Mock) {

  return Backbone.Router.extend({
    routes: {
      "movies/:id": "showMovie",
      "": "index"
    },

    index: function() {

    },
    showMovie: function() {

    }

  });
});
```

Besides monitoring URL changes, the router must fetch data and render the views. For development, we also introduce a reference to our mock setup. Let's start setting up the collections next.

Thorax.Collection

Once the router is in place, it is time to setup a movies collection. Similarly to the router, you can scaffold a Movies collection with the generator:

```
$ yo thorax:collection movies
```

which results in:

```
create js/collections/movies.js
create test/collections/movies.spec.js
```

We now fill in the collection, which is very similar to a Backbone.Collection, and all we do right now is set the URL:

```
define(['collection'], function (Collection) {
  return Collection.extend({
    name: 'movies',
    url: '/api/movies'
  });
});
```

A small difference between a Backbone collection and a Thorax collection is that a Thorax collection can guard multiple fetches with a FetchQueue. This prevents the browser from doing HTTP requests when we can still "live" with the current data. This can be important for mobile applications.

In the router, let's fetch the mock data from the browser as a first test. For this, we include the collection as dependency in the Movies router. The router then becomes:

```
define([
  'backbone',
  'mocks',
  'collections/movies'
], function (Backbone, Mock, MoviesCollection) {
  var movies;

  return Backbone.Router.extend({
    routes: {
      "movies/:id": "showMovie",
      "": "index"
    },
    index: function() {
      movies = new Movies();
      movies.on("all", function(ev) { console.log(ev) });
      movies.fetch({success: function(results) {
        console.log(results);
      }, fail: function() {
        console.log("fallback");
        }
      });
    },
    showMovie: function() {
    }
  });
});
```

To see some action, let's start up the application with Grunt:

```
$ grunt
```

Then, we can test that the collection works by going to *http://0.0.0.0:8000/*. The browser console reveals the following:

```
load:start
request
reset
load:end
sync
```

So, besides the Backbone.js reset and sync, we also see events `load:start` and `load:end`. These events are especially useful to show and hide loading messages and keep loading data with routes in sync.

 Thorax provides a number of enhancements to simplify synchronization of state with the DOM. On one side, you get some support for easier data binding, which is needed when dealing with inputs from HTML forms. On the other side, Thorax has helpers as `bindTo Route`, where slow (mobile) data connection can guard against state changes.

Now that we have movies data, let's continue to rendering movies.

Rendering

Thorax.js supports helpers from Handlebars.js and a number of special view helpers, so rendering advanced views becomes very easy.

First, we prepare the root view, which gives us a basic layout for the application. We use a basic root layout derived from the HelloWorld example:

```
<header>
  <a href="#">Munich Cinema</a>
</header>

<section class="thorax-container thorax-wrapper">
  <div class="thorax-primary">
      {{layout-element}}
  </div>
</section>

<footer>
  <ul>
    <li><a href="credits">Some credits</a></li>
  </ul>
</footer>
```

The `layout-element` that is enclosed in double curly braces is a Thorax view helper and acts as main point to rendering the views. If you inspect the source code of `layout-view`, you will see some Handlebars code applied behind the scenes.

The idea of a layout is similar to a master template that is shared across multiple views. We can also embed a header and view child with view helpers as follows:

```
<header>
  {{view header}}
</header>
```

With this, we easily can render child views that are properties on the parent views. We reference these child views as follows:

```
var RootView = LayoutView.extend({
  name: 'root',
  template: rootTemplate,
  initialize: function() {
    this.header = new Header();
  }
});
```

For the index and showMovie actions in the router, we need to render a list of movies and the details, so let's add them:

```
$ yo thorax:view movies/index
$ yo thorax:view movies/show
```

Then, in the *js/views/movies/index.hbs* file, we render the collection of movies with:

```
<h2>The latest movies</h2>
{{#collection}}
  {{#link "movies/{{id}}" expand-tokens=true}}
    {{ title }}
  {/link}
{{/collection}}
```

By using view helpers from Thorax and Handlebars, our views become more readable, and it's easier to embed child views, too. In this example, you use the collection view helper, which can also facilitate filtering.

 Thorax has more strategies to improve working with Backbone views. For example, Thorax provides an extended event hash to simplify binding of common events from models and collections. Also, Thorax provides view helpers to deal with user input from forms.

In order to render the movies, we must connect the MovieView with a Movies collection in the router with:

```
define([
  'backbone',
  'mocks',
  'collections/movies',
  'views/root',
  'views/movies/index'
], function (Backbone, Mock, MoviesCollection, RootView, IndexView) {
  var collection;
```

```
    if (!collection) {
      collection = new MoviesCollection();
      Mock.start();
      console.log("*** Mock movies API ***");
    }

    return Backbone.Router.extend({
      routes: {
        "movies/;id": "showMovie",
        "": "index"
      },
      index: function() {
        var view;
        collection.fetch({success: function(result) {
          view = new IndexView({collection: collection});
          RootView.getInstance().setView(view);
        }});
      },
      showMovie: function() {
      }
    });
  });
```

When we now go to the browser main page, you should see a working index view. When we click on a movie, nothing yet happens unless we add the rendering of showMovie.

So, we can wire up the show view route in *app/routers/browser.js*:

```
showMovie: function(id) {
  var movie = collection.get(id);
  var view = new ShowMovie({model: movie});
  RootView.getInstance().setView(view);
}
```

Conclusion

This chapter covered the basics of the Yeoman generator for Thorax. Based on RequireJS, you saw how a large Backbone application can be structured and how using Handlebars view helpers of Thorax can simplify the setup of views. Importantly, you saw how the layout-element can be used to place a child view in a layout. Then, you saw how to place sub-views, such as a header and footer, with the view helper.

Thorax offers additional features, such as support for better loading of data and dealing with inputs from user forms. Also, Thorax can provide support for automated tests. And, as with any Backbone project, you can keep your options open to easily replace building blocks when the requirements on your application change.

Developing with JavaScript

For client-side application development, a good understanding of JavaScript is necessary. JavaScript is a dynamic, object-oriented language. For an in-depth background, you might want to refer to some of the books listed in the Preface. This appendix provides a short overview on getting started with Node.js and a short refresher on the role of Underscore and jQuery.

Installing Node

Node.js is based on Google's V8 library, which is written in C++. Node.js runs on all major operating systems.

Starting with Mac OS, an easy approach to install Node.js is by using Homebrew. Homebrew is a package manager for Mac OS (see *http://brew.sh/* for basic installation instructions).

Once Homebrew is installed, you can run the following:

```
$ brew upgrade
$ brew install node
```

Alternatively, you can visit the download page (*http://nodejs.org/download/*).

Here, you also find the Node versions for Windows and source code packages.

If you are running an Ubuntu or Debian flavor of Linux, you can install Node.js with:

```
sudo apt-get install build-essential libssl-dev curl git-core
sudo apt-get install nodejs
```

If you need to run different versions of Node.js (e.g., if you are dealing with constraints in production), you might want to have a look at NVM (*https://github.com/creationix/nvm*). With NVM, you can easily switch between versions of Node.js.

Getting Functional with Underscore.js

Because JavaScript in its old standard didn't have helpers for dealing with enumerators, Underscore.js was born. Underscore.js provides many nifty JavaScript shortcuts and is also a core dependency of Backbone.js. Underscore.js derives many ideas from functional programming.

In functional programming, we can easily extract meta information from data structures, or chain operations on data structures independent from the data itself. This flexibility is achieved by passing functions as arguments to other functions, often under the concept of higher-level functions.

The main goal of the Underscore.js library is to provide a set of abstractions to transform and aggregate data structures. Underscore.js comes with excellent documentation (*http://underscorejs.org/*).

After loading the library, we obtain a helper to the global namespace of the browser window. To get a feeling of what the shortcut can do, we can look at some examples.

 Due to the success of Underscore.js, there are a number of derivatives from the original library. First, in underscore-contrib (*http://documentcloud.github.io/underscore-contrib/*), a lot more ideas from functional programming are made possible in JavaScript. Another variation can be found in underscore.string (*https://github.com/epeli/underscore.string*). This library provides a number of default string transformations Last, there is underscore-cli (*https://github.com/ddopson/underscore-cli*), which provides helpers to transform JSON from the command line.

Collections and Arrays

Some of the most important helpers from Underscore.js are improvements in dealing with collections. The helpers that are provided from Underscore.js will look familiar to Ruby developers. We need to load underscore into the console.

Let's build a movies list:

```
var midnight_in_paris = {title: "Midnight in Paris"};
var indiana_jones = {title: "Indiana Jones"};
var movies = [midnight_in_paris, indiana_jones]
var show = function(movie) { console.log(movie.title); }
_.each(movies, show);   // ❶
```

For the _.each() helper, we pass in an array and a function that operates on the members of the list. The output of (1) will then look like:

```
"Midnight in Paris"
"Indiana Jones"
```

Next, Underscore.js helps in bringing objects into a new form. For example, with _.map(), we can extract a list of titles from a movies list:

```
var movie_titles = _.map(movies, function(movie) {
  return movie.title;
});
console.log(movie_titles);
```

With _.reduce(), we can, for example, sum up numbers in a list:

```
_.reduce(movies, function(actor_no, movie) {
    return actor_no + movie.actors.length
  },
0);
```

With Underscore.js, it also is easy to make the union of two sets:

```
var allGenres = _.union(midnight_in_paris.genres, indiana_jones.genres); // (3)
console.log(allGenres);
```

Functions

We mentioned the role of context in JavaScript a few times already. Because functions can be executed from different contexts, it is often helpful to explicitly bind a context to a function. One option to do this can be Underscore's bind and bindAll functions. Starting with ECMAScript 5, you can also use a new function called Function.proto type.bind that can natively enforce a context.

The idea of bind can be seen as follows:

```
announceMovie = _.bind(announceMovie, {title: 'The Artist'});
announceMovie()
Coming next: The Artist
```

So, we can call a function, without passing an argument or referencing the outer context. These kinds of shortcuts allow us to encapsulate code and data (e.g., to be used in callbacks).

For example, if title changes or is undefined for a certain function context, the method announceMovie still uses the object that was bound. So:

```
name = 'Taxi Driver'
setTimeout(announceMovie, 1000);
```

still results in:

```
Coming next: The Artist
```

Another helper from Underscore is invoke:

```
var complete = _.invoke([movies, genres], 'fetch', {async: false});
```

With this, functions can be invoked on a list of objects, such as the array [movies, genres] discussed earlier.

Objects

From the perspective of code organization, it is often necessary to share functions across multiple objects. This would be difficult if we could only use JavaScript prototype inheritance. Underscore.js provides some other ways to customize the interfaces of objects. For example, there is extend, which allows us to copy properties from one object onto another:

```
var movieReview = _.extend(midnight_in_paris,
                          { reviewer: 'anne', description: '...'});
console.log(movieReview);
```

We now have the properties from the movie midnight_in_paris copied onto the movieReview object.

Apart from new ways to customize interfaces of objects, Underscore.js provides some easy ways to introspect objects.

For example, values() would just return the values of object properties:

```
var summary = _.values(midnight_in_paris);
console.log(summary);
```

Utility

The last group of helpers from Underscore.js are just plain utility functions.

First, there are helpers to render objects within templates. The general idea is the following:

```
var welcome = _.template("Welcome, <%= name %>!");
console.log(welcome({name: 'patrick'}));

Welcome, patrick!
```

jQuery Basics

Backbone.js applications will require a library to modify the nodes in the DOM and to work with Ajax requests out of the browser. Therefore, Backbone.js depends on a library like jQuery or Zepto.

For a basic understanding of jQuery, check out *jQuery Cookbook* by Cody Lindley (O'Reilly, 2009) or *Learning from jQuery* by Callum Macrae (O'Reilly, 2013).

The short review that follows is for making the jump from server-side application development to client-side easier. In essence, jQuery is a wrapper around the DOM, and we start the discussion there.

Selecting Elements

To understand the purpose of jQuery, let's look at what web browsers do. Web browsers parse HTML into the so-called Document Object Model (DOM). The DOM is a browser's internal representation of HTML and is made up of nodes. After the HTML is parsed into nodes, the nodes are fed into the browser's layout engine before a web page is displayed to the user.

There are different types of DOM nodes to represent HTML tags. For example, let's look at the following HTML construct:

```
<div id="movie" class="selected">The Artist</div>
```

Here, an element with attributes id and class encloses a text element. The nodes could be selected with JavaScript by using:

```
document.getElementById('movie')
document.getElementByTag('div')
```

Without jQuery, walking through a list of nodes or selecting a node from a relative position would be not so easy. With jQuery, selecting nodes can be done:

```
$('#movie')
$('#movies article:last')
```

Another important syntax for selecting a node is matching attributes of tags, like:

```
$('article[data-id=1]')
```

This matches article nodes with the attribute data-id set to 1.

There is a small difference between selecting DOM nodes with pure JavaScript or with jQuery: with pure JavaScript, we merely obtain a representation of a node in JavaScript. With jQuery, we actually obtain a jQuery wrapper around a node providing us again with jQuery functionality. A jQuery wrapped enables:

Collection helpers
> When we select nodes from a list. for example, we can directly operate on the list items. For example, we can use $(*#movies div*).hide() to hide all movies instead of looping over the nodes manually.

Chaining methods
> Wrapping nodes with jQuery allows us to chain operations on a node. For example, we can toggle a CSS class and change the text value all at once:

```
$("#movies").first().css('background', 'green').text('a test')
```

Creating DOM nodes is also easier with jQuery. Instead of writing:

```
var movie = document.createElement('div');
movie.innerHTML = 'The Artist';
```

we can simply use the following:

```
var movie = $('<article>The Artist</article>');
```

Modifying the content of DOM nodes can be done with jQuery as follows:

```
movie.html('The Piano');
```

or:

```
movie.text('Taxi Driver');
```

For performance reasons, it is important to realize that html also does syntax checking operations and can be slower than simply calling the value of the innerHTML property.

Working with Events

Basically, an event consists of an event type and a node in the DOM where the event occurred. Handling events is one of the most complicated aspects of programming a web browser with JavaScript. It's not just that various browsers have slightly different ways to attach event handlers to nodes in the DOM, but also that removing these handlers makes the life of a programmer difficult at times.

Without jQuery, we can attach an event handler directly on an element with:

```
var element = document.getElementById('movie');
element.onclick = function() {
  // ... process the click
}
```

or by registering an event listener on a node with:

```
document.addEventListener(node, handler);
```

In jQuery, there are is a short syntax for adding handlers to certain event types on nodes. For example, for a click event, you can use:

```
$('#movie').on('click', function(ev) {
  // ... process the click
}
```

A common problem with events is *event bubbling*. Multiple nodes will capture an event if events are not prevented to pass from children nodes to their parents. Event bubbling can be prevented with jQuery with:

```
event.preventDefault();
```

Also, when new nodes are created, it is a common mistake to duplicate unwanted event handlers (e.g., for submitting a form). It is important to clean up events from "old" nodes before new nodes are inserted.

Ajax

For quite some years, loading new content with JavaScript into the browser was rather difficult. Things changed when the XMLHttpRequest object was introduced into the DOM.

The name XMLHttpRequest is confusing at first, because it can load any content (not only XML) and it can also talk HTTPS (not only HTTP). In order to send an HTTP request from JavaScript, we must set the request type, the URL, the header, and the request parameters on a XMLHttpRequest object. We then wait for a response event and parse the received data accordingly.

By using jQuery, we obtain some syntactic sugar around this process and a uniform behavior across most browsers. Although Backbone.js comes with a wrapper for Ajax, it is instructive to look at the jQuery Ajax API.

Let's look at how to load additional content with the jQuery Ajax API. For example, we might have a select box where we want to load details of the selected movie. We could do this as follows:

```
<html>
  <head>
    <script src="/js/libs/jquery/jquery.js"></script>
    <script>
      $(document).ready(function() {
        // ... here comes the Ajax magic

      });
    </script>
  </head>
<body>
  <form action="#" id="movies">
      <p>Select a movie:</p>
      <select name="title" id="movielist" size="1">
        <option data-id='1'>The Artist</option>
        <option data-id='2'>Taxi Driver</option>
        <option data-id='3'>La Dolce Vita</option>
      </select>
  </form>

  <div id="movieDetails">
  </div>
</body>
</html>
```

We can detect a change of the selected movie with a simple event handler attached to the change event. We then load the movie details with Ajax as follows:

```
$(function(){
  $('#movielist').change(function() {
      var title = $(this).val();
      var id = $(this).data('id');
      $('#movieDetails').load('movies.json', { title: title });
    }).change();
});
```

Index

We'd like to hear your suggestions for improving our indexes. Send email to index@oreilly.com.

Windows, Node.js installation, 161
wireframes
    benefits of, 21
    creating, 20
workflow, automation of (see build automation)

X

XMLHttpRequest object, 167

Y

Yeoman
    application directory, 144

benefits of, 140, 142
installation of, 142
running, 143

Z

Zepto library, 2, 164

About the Author

Before discovering software development for web applications with Java and Ruby in 2008, **Patrick Mulder** mainly worked as a software engineer on measurement equipment and electronic devices. Web development allowed him to learn about networks and linking documents, but working with measurement equipment gave him an appreciation for the many forms data can have. Not for nothing, Tim Berners-Lee invented large parts of the WWW while working at CERN, a European research organization for particle physics.

Yet, after programming with C, C++, Python, Ruby, and Java, learning Backbone.js proved difficult, as Patrick did not have much experience with the "nonblocking" behavior of JavaScript when he started working with Backbone. Luckily, he teamed up with a JavaScript developer who taught him the differences of JavaScript from other programming languages. In the meantime, Patrick is convinced that JavaScript and Backbone are just great to explore data and interfaces for the Web.

Patrick likes blogging at *http://thinkingonthinking.com*, and has a passion for data-driven interfaces and data in general. After working in big and small software companies, he now works as a freelance software consultant, focusing on JavaScript, web interfaces, and measurement systems.

Colophon

The animal on the cover of *Full Stack Web Development with Backbone.js* is a pipe fish (*Syngnathinae*), which is a unique, slender, long-bodied fish with rings of bony armor along its body. These animals are related to seahorses, and similarities can be seen in the length and shape of their snouts. They have a single dorsal fin and most have a small tail fin. There are nearly 200 species and they range in size from 1 to 26 inches.

Pipe fish don't have large fins and have a rigid body structure, making them slow swimmers. Instead, they rely on camouflage to avoid detection. There are even a few species of pipe fish that have prehensile tails for grabbing and holding plants. Pipe fish come in a wide range of patterns and colors ranging from drab to brightly colored, and there are even some that can change their color in order to match their surroundings.

The pipe fish is typically found in a tropical or subtropical region. While most pipe fish live in saltwater environments, some have been known to enter and survive in freshwater environments. Pipe fish, like their seahorse relatives, leave most of the parenting duties to the male, which provides all of the care for its offspring, supplying them with nutrients and oxygen through a placenta-like connection.

The cover image is from Lydekker's Natural History. The cover fonts are URW Typewriter and Guardian Sans. The text font is Adobe Minion Pro; the heading font is Adobe Myriad Condensed; and the code font is Dalton Maag's Ubuntu Mono.

Get even more for your money.

Join the O'Reilly Community, and register the O'Reilly books you own. It's free, and you'll get:

- $4.99 ebook upgrade offer
- 40% upgrade offer on O'Reilly print books
- Membership discounts on books and events
- Free lifetime updates to ebooks and videos
- Multiple ebook formats, DRM FREE
- Participation in the O'Reilly community
- Newsletters
- Account management
- 100% Satisfaction Guarantee

Signing up is easy:

1. Go to: oreilly.com/go/register
2. Create an O'Reilly login.
3. Provide your address.
4. Register your books.

Note: English-language books only

To order books online:
oreilly.com/store

For questions about products or an order:
orders@oreilly.com

To sign up to get topic-specific email announcements and/or news about upcoming books, conferences, special offers, and new technologies:
elists@oreilly.com

For technical questions about book content:
booktech@oreilly.com

To submit new book proposals to our editors:
proposals@oreilly.com

O'Reilly books are available in multiple DRM-free ebook formats. For more information:
oreilly.com/ebooks

Ingram Content Group UK Ltd.
Milton Keynes UK
UKHW031839310323
419486UK00009B/873